HOW TO DO
PRACTICALLY
EVERYTHING
FOR
PRACTICALLY
NOTHING

NICOLE PARTON

How to Do Practically Everything for Practically Nothing

DECORATIONS BY
John Spencer

WORLD'S WORK

First published in Canada, by *The Vancouver Sun*,
in two volumes, 1980 and 1981
Published in Great Britain 1983 by
World's Work Ltd
The Windmill Press
Kingswood, Tadworth, Surrey

Printed in Great Britain by
Billing and Sons Ltd., London and Worcester

ISBN 0437 12695 1

TABLE OF EQUIVALENTS

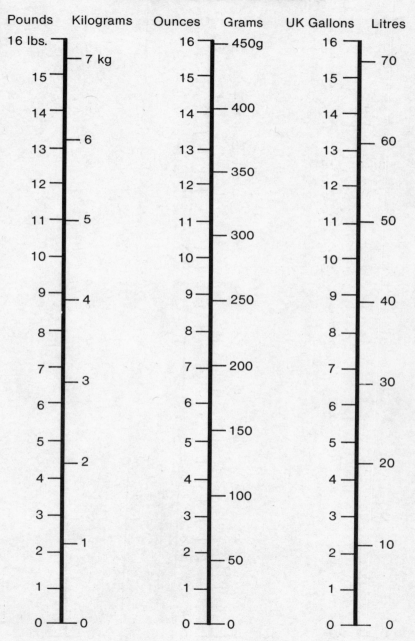

TABLE OF EQUIVALENTS

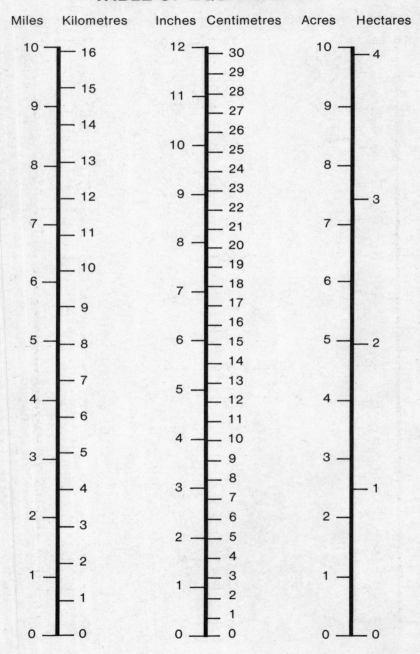

Miles	Kilometres	Inches	Centimetres	Acres	Hectares

TABLE OF EQUIVALENTS

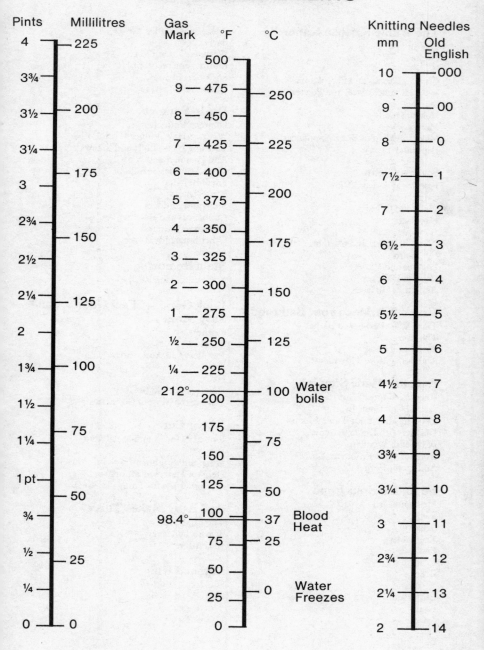

Pints	Millilitres
4	225
3¾	
3½	200
3¼	
3	175
2¾	
2½	150
2¼	125
2	
1¾	100
1½	
1¼	75
1pt	
¾	50
½	25
¼	
0	0

Gas Mark	°F	°C	
	500		
9	475	250	
8	450		
7	425	225	
6	400		
5	375	200	
4	350		
3	325	175	
2	300	150	
1	275		
½	250	125	
¼	225		
212°	200	100	Water boils
	175		
	150	75	
	125	50	
98.4°	100	37	Blood Heat
	75	25	
	50		
	25	0	Water Freezes
	0		

Knitting Needles mm	Old English
10	000
9	00
8	0
7½	1
7	2
6½	3
6	4
5½	5
5	6
4½	7
4	8
3¾	9
3¼	10
3	11
2¾	12
2¼	13
2	14

CONTENTS

Pet's Corner
Cats
Dogs
Cage Birds
Garden Birds
And Other Household Pets

Car Sense
Emergencies
Cleaning
Coping in the Freeze-up
Other Useful Tips
And Don't Forget

Gardening Time
Seeds
Young Plants
Shrubs
Potting Compost and Fertilizers
Weeding
Pest Control
Cut and Dried Flowers
Houseplants
Storage
And Other Gardeners' Secrets

Festive Occasions
Christmas
Birthdays
Easter and Hallowe'en
General Party Tips

And The Rest
Posting Parcels
Lost and Found
Looking after Valuables
Beating the Cold Weather
Calculations Made Easy
Postscript

The Whole Kitchen Kaboodle

Pots and Pans

- Glass casserole lids need less cleaning if they're lightly coated with vegetable oil or marg before you bake or stew. Cooked-on splatters wash off like a charm.

- Clean your roasting pan as you snooze. Spray it with oven cleaner and forget it, rinsing it clean the morning after.

- Clean even the grimiest cast iron frying pan but spare the elbow grease. Throw it into your oven the next time you're ready to flick on the self-cleaning cycle.

- A badly burned saucepan will often clean itself if you boil a cut-up onion in it. The burned bits should float to the top of the pan.

- Here's a fast way to clean copper-bottom pans. The next time you cook potatoes, save the water. Any copper soaked in it will emerge sparkling clean and almost like new . . . OR . . . sprinkle salt on a wedge of lemon, using it like a scouring pad . . . OR . . . make a paste of cigar ashes and water, rubbing it into the metal . . . OR . . . mix equal parts of flour and salt with enough white vinegar to make a paste. Then stand back and admire the shine.

- Clean and shine copper-bottom saucepans with rhubarb leaves fresh from the garden. Chop the leaves into several small pieces and cover with boiling water in a large old pot. Put copper-bottom pan to be cleaned into the larger pot with the rhubarb solution, simmering 10 to 15 minutes (a little water in the copper-bottom pot will hold it in place). Dull copper will shine without polishing in about 5 minutes, but badly-crusted spots may not come clean.

The stalk works just as well, but why waste the edible part?

■ If you run out of copper polish, ketchup will do the job.

■ Clean copper with a mixture of 1 tbsp. flour, 1 tbsp. salt, and 1 tbsp. vinegar.

■ Clean brass with buttermilk or rub it with a cut lemon. It works!

■ Rust and grime will often lift off baking tins that have been well greased and heated in a 350 deg. F. oven for 10 to 15 min. before cleansing ... OR ... use a cut raw potato, dipped in cleaning powder.

■ Baking tins will never rust at all, some folks say, if you grease and heat them for about 15 min. before using them the first time.

■ A burnt grill pan will scrub out with less work if you apply a paste of bicarbonate of soda and water to it and allow it to stand several hours or overnight. This also works on stainless steel saucepans; for aluminium pans, use a cream-of-tartar-and-water-solution.

■ Hard-to-clean saucepans wash out easily if you boil any leaves from the garden in them for 15 to 20 minutes. Use a small amount of water and cover the pot.

■ Scour Teflon pans without scratching by using an old expired credit card as a scraper.

■ Pots won't boil dry if you toss a couple of marbles into the bubbling water below the steamer insert or in the bottom half of your double boiler. As the level of water in the pan drops, you'll hear them bounce.

■ The stubborn dirt on the bottom of your electric frying pan will lift off with an application of oven cleaner (allow to stand several minutes before scrubbing) ... OR ... by soaking in a paste made from powdered dishwashing detergent and water.

Ovens

- Sop up that pool of grease in your oven. Sprinkle it with salt while the oven is warm, whisking off with a stiff brush after the oven has cooled.

- Clean the interior of your microwave oven without scratching the finish. Sift a little bicarbonate of soda on a damp sponge, and go to it.

- Prevent splatters as you're frying. Up-end a metal colander over the pan . . . OR . . . sprinkle a little salt into the grease.

- Oven cleanings are simpler if you put a shallow dish of ammonia and water inside immediately after roasting anything that splatters. Allow to stand overnight; in the morning, wash out with hot, soapy water to which a few drops of vinegar have been added.

Fridges

- Check if the rubber gasket seal on your fridge or freezer needs replacing. Shut the door on a lit torch. If you can see light escaping, cold air is escaping, too, boosting your energy costs. Or shut the fridge door on a protruding slip of paper. If you can slide the paper out, it's time to replace the seal.

- Your fridge will operate more efficiently if it stands away from heat sources (including direct sunlight) and if you give its coils and grates an occasional vacuum.

1

Glasses, Carafes and Percolators

- Banish stains from the bottom of slim-necked wine decanters. Pour warm water into the container, add a crushed eggshell, and shake vigorously ... OR ... plop in a denture tablet and a little warm water ... OR ... add a handful of raw rice and a splash of vinegar, and shake.

- Clouded crystal can sometimes be cleaned if covered with a layer of damp potato peelings and allowed to stand undisturbed for 24 hours. Wash and rinse in cool water.

- Hand-washed crystal is less likely to chip if you lay a dishcloth on the bottom of the sink in which you wash each piece. Add 2 tbsp. of ammonia to the rinse water, and you won't have any streaks, either.

- And if you should nick a crystal glass, try filing the chip with an emery board.

- Clean stained plastic coffee filter cones by soaking them in warm water to which you've added a pinch of powdered dishwashing detergent.

- Clean wine bottles and carafes with warm water and an ounce of baking soda ... OR ... by popping in a denture tablet and allowing to dissolve in warm water.

- Your glasses will dry spot-free if you add a little vinegar to your dishwasher's rinse cycle.

- Clean stained coffee percs and enamel pans with a solution of one part liquid chlorine bleach to two parts water. Let stand in perc 5 min., shaking well to coat filter and stem. Use weekly, being sure to rinse percolator thoroughly after cleaning. This solution may be stored in a glass jar for re-use.

- Clean your coffee perc by running it through its regular cycle with 2 tbsp. baking soda and hot soapy water, and then running it through again with hot clear water.

- Tea and coffee stains will lift off your delicate china cups if you rub the insides of each with a damp cloth sprinkled with bicarbonate of soda ... OR ... with salt.

- Clean discoloured vases like new by dropping in a denture tablet ... OR ... by adding a few bits of finely chopped potato and ½ cup vinegar and allowing to stand several minutes. Wash in warm sudsy water and rinse.

Silver, Stainless Steel and Pewter

- Give the fluted border of your best silver a super shine. Plug in your old electric toothbrush, and get gleaming.

- Clean stainless steel cutlery with a paste of ground tailor's chalk and water; wash as usual. Never use silver cleaners or solvents on stainless steel.

- To clean aluminum cutlery, dunk in a pot of boiling water to which you've added 2 tsp. cream of tartar.

1

- Remove stains and rust from a carbon-steel knife blade by rubbing with a wide cork moistened with onion juice, or with a cut onion.

- Shine up your sterling silver. Soak it in sour milk overnight.

- Polish brass with Worcester sauce.

- Polish tin with a cut onion and a dry cloth.

- The simplest way to clean silver is to boil it in an old aluminum pot with 1 tbsp. salt and 1 tbsp. bicarbonate of soda added to each quart of water. The tarnish will coat the pot and your silver will gleam.

- Stored silverware won't tarnish if you tuck a small piece of alum into your silver chest.

- Remove egg stains from silverware by rubbing liberally with salt sprinkled on a clean dry cloth. Rinse and dry immediately lest the salt corrode your silver.

- Pewter polishes up nicely with a dab of toothpaste ... OR ... a couple of cabbage leaves.

- Buff and polish chrome with a sprinkle of dry bicarbonate of soda on a dry cloth ... OR ... with dampened aluminium foil. The chrome will shine and the foil will turn black.

- Your stainless steel kitchen sink will sparkle if you scour it with soda water ... make sure it hasn't lost its fizz.

Storage

- You'll always know what's in your deep freeze if you tape a simple inventory card to the door. If you have five apple pies, for example, count them like this: / / / / /. If you bake two, just cross those off: XX / / /. This method works beautifully for anything in the freezer.

- Store biscuits intended for the freezer in empty foil or wax paper cartons.

- Tuck electrical appliance cords and extensions into toilet tissue tubes, labelling each by length and by which cord fits which appliance.

- Paper bags will look neater if they're held by a large clip mounted to the inside of your broom cupboard.

- Store dusters, waxes, and cleaning materials in an old shoe bag hung inside the door of your broom cupboard. Helps keep things organized and tidy.

- Store iron-on mending tape in an adhesive tape dispenser.

Help at Hand

- Unclog your kitchen sink by pouring a full cup of salt and a full cup of bicarbonate of soda down the drain, dousing both with a kettle of boiling water. Grease will dissolve with this treatment.

- Replace a leaky sink plug with a plastic yogurt lid. This won't drain your budget, either.

- Extinguish greasy kitchen fires by throwing baking soda on the flames.

1

- You can often salvage scorched food, keeping it from tasting burnt, by plunging the pan into cold water before transferring the food to a second pan to resume cooking.

- Dissolve lime scales from kettles and irons with full strength vinegar. Boil in appliance briefly, then allow to stand overnight.

Make the Most of Your Appliances

- A new yard broom will last longer if you soak it in a pail of very hot water to which you've added 1 tbsp. white vinegar or salt. This toughens the straw.

- Squeezy mops will remain moist and supple if you tie a plastic bag over the sponge part after using.

- Scouring pads will never rust if you sprinkle a little bicarbonate of soda in the bottom of the dish in which they're stored.

- Dirty or smelly dishcloth? Toss it into the dishwasher along with your load of dishes, making sure it won't slip down onto the revolving spray arm. It should come out clean and sweet.

- Save energy by turning your dishwasher off just as the drying cycle begins, and allowing your dishes to air-dry.

Money Savers

- Double the life of soap-filled scouring pads by cutting them in half.

- Make your own pot scrubbers by rolling up two plastic mesh bags (the kind onions come in are perfect) and sewing both ends.

- Freeze produce or pack sandwiches in washed-out plastic bread bags.

- Renew a fraying rubber spatula by trimming it with scissors.

- Disguise a crack in your favourite dish by simmering it in sweet milk for 45 min. The dish will look almost new.

- Replace a broken pot lid knob with a large cork – it won't transmit heat.

- Replace a torn mate to a pair of rubber gloves by turning a saved old glove inside out.

Hints and Tips

- Carrier bags used for refuse won't leak if they're lined with an opened plastic egg carton.

- Remove plastic that has melted onto your toaster or waffle iron. Swab it away with nail polish remover or a little bicarbonate of soda applied to a damp cloth, and watch it disappear without any scratches.

- Remove the sticky adhesive left from gummy price tags. A little hairspray or a dab of clear nail polish remover act like magic – but caution! The nail polish remover may damage some plastics.

1

- Soak wet flour from your dish-cloth. Add a pinch of bicarbonate of soda to the water.

- Dust crumbs from your tablecloth without having to remove and shake it. Scissor a foil pie plate in two, using the smaller section to sweep and the other to collect.

- Formica will gleam if it's polished with sparkly soda water.

- Loosen paper stuck to your counter top with a little olive oil.

- Oil and syrup bottles won't leave a sticky ring in your kitchen cupboard if you put yoghurt or cottage cheese lids under them.

- Cool extra baking on inverted bun tins if you're short of racks. A slightly raised oven rack is good, too.

- Extend your small kitchen work area by pulling a drawer part way out and topping with a baking sheet.

- You'll never dump a short drawer on the floor again if you paint the last couple of inches at the top glide bright red. That's your signal to stop pulling.

- China plates won't chip as you put them away if you place a paper towel between each.

- Splash-proof often-used recipes by slipping them into a bag ... OR ... inverting a glass pie plate over them ... OR ... laying them under the clear plastic pages of a photo album.

- Cleaning your chest freezer is easier on the back if you use a long-handled sponge mop to soak up every last puddle.

2

Sweep Clean

Floors – Wood and Vinyl

- Spilled grease can easily be scraped off a kitchen floor if you harden the mess with ice water, first.

- Rub black heel marks from your vinyl floors by swabbing with a squirt of toothpaste and a damp cloth. This works on crayon marks, too, as does lemon extract, paste floor wax, or silver polish.

- Clean stubborn stains from wooden floors. Use a fine steel wool dampened with turpentine.

- Why buy wax stripper when you can make it for pennies? Combine 5 cups warm water, 1 cup powdered laundry detergent, and ¾ cup ammonia. Rinse before reapplying wax.

- Clean and condition your hardwood floors. Combine 4 cups liquid paraffin from the chemist with 1 cup inexpensive salad oil. Add ¼ cup ammonia and ½ cup turpentine, storing well out of children's reach. This concentrate should be diluted with 4 parts water to 1 part cleaner/conditioner before rubbing onto floors. No rinsing needed.

2

- Give your floors a light buff and save money on wax by adding a few drops of regular liquid floor wax to warm water, going over your floors with this instead of full-strength liquid wax. This method should not be used on hardwood floors.

- Floor boards won't squeak if they're dusted with talcum powder.

- Stop a wooden floor from squeaking. Work powdered graphite between the boards or squirt a fews drops of washing up liquid between any cracks you see.

- Remove a badly marked floor tile by using your sunlamp to soften the glue.

- Replacement floor tiles drop into place snugly after brief heating with the flame of a propane torch.

- Lay floor tiles flat. Use your rolling pin. Because your weight is evenly distributed while you roll, the glue won't be thick in one spot and patchy in another.

- Tubular metal chairs won't scratch your floors if you take extra precautions with the legs' plastic protector caps. Tuck a metal washer (the same diameter as each chair leg) into each plastic cap, refitting the caps on the chairs. The caps will last far longer – so will your floors.

Carpet Care

- Vacuuming stair treads is child's play when you use a toy sweeper – it's just the right size.

- Faded carpets will look brighter if you liberally sprinkle salt on them, allow it to lie undisturbed for about an hour, and then vacuum.

- Remove damp mud spots from your carpet by sprinkling with salt, allowing to set for an hour, and then vacuuming.

- Lift candle wax stains from your rugs by placing a generous chunk of brown paper bag over the stain and heating with a warm iron, making sure the iron doesn't touch the

2

carpet lest it melt the pile. The paper should absorb the blob of wax.

- Grease stains will vanish from a carpet sprinkled with bicarbonate of soda and allowed to rest one hour before vacuuming.

- Red wine stains on your rug? Quick! Grab the white wine. One cancels out the other – but don't try the reverse should you spill some white wine first.

- Try this spot remover on your carpet – a shot of shaving cream. Try it in a hidden corner, first, rinsing well.

- Large rugs won't slide and buckle over a carpet if you stitch a giant mesh fishing net to the backing of the top rug.

- Carpet edges won't curl if you sew a cardboard "L" shape in each corner.

- Shapeless rugs look snappier and lie flatter if you apply several coats of shellac to the backing, allowing ample drying time between each coat.

- Scatter rugs won't slip if you line the edge of the backing with leftover weather stripping, pressing the sticky side to the backing ... OR ... throw a kitchen drain mat or rubber bath mat underneath. This is especially good in icy weather, when you'd like a non-skid outdoor mat.

- To find tiny articles lost on the floor or in the pile of your rug, slip an old stocking over the nozzle of your vacuum cleaner preventing the object from entering the tube.

- Save your rugs while wet boots drip. A split plastic laundry basket makes an excellent holder. Just trim down the sides; tuck into the hall cupboard when not in use.

Walls and Ceilings

- Want to scrub a ceiling in double quick time? Use a sponge-mop.

23

2

- Green mildew spots will vanish from white stucco sprayed with undiluted chlorine bleach.

- Kids' wax crayon marks will lift off walls rubbed gently with a little toothpaste. But don't try this on flocked wallpapers, please.

- Clean painted walls and woodwork with this mild solution. Combine 2 cups warm water, 1 tsp. bicarbonate of soda, 4 tsp. ammonia, and 2 tsp. white vinegar, pouring into a squeezy bottle. Squirt on dirt, rinsing with cool water.

- Painted surfaces can also be cleaned with this solution. Combine 5 cups warm water, ¼ cup washing soda, ¼ cup white vinegar, and ½ cup ammonia. Rinse off with cool, clear water.

- Can't wash your wallpaper? Try this cleaner. Combine 2 cups flour, 2 tbsp. salt, and 2 tbsp. powdered ammonia, mixing well. Add 2 cups water, 2 tbsp. white vinegar, and 2 tbsp. paraffin oil until mixture is like a paste. Cook, stirring constantly, over medium heat, until very thick. Remove from heat and cool, pinching off small pieces and rolling these over wallpaper with an up-and-down motion, picking up the dirt as you go.

Fireplaces

- Glass-screened fireplace doors will look like new if you use a little oven cleaner on those smoke stains. Let it work for several minutes before wiping it off with a clean, damp cloth. Be sure to wear rubber gloves – oven cleaner is caustic ... OR ... rub the smoke stains with a dampened cloth and a little fireplace ash, drying with a lint-free cloth.

- Smoke stains will fade from a stone-faced fireplace if they're gently rubbed with a soft india rubber.

- Remove stains from marble by rubbing gently with a paste of water, bicarbonate of soda, and a little lemon juice.

- Clean fireplace tongs, shovels, and screens with a solution of 1 part bicarbonate of soda to 5 parts water. Rinse with cool, clear water, polishing with a soft cloth. You can soak fireplace broom bristles in this solution, too.

- Your slate hearth will have a pleasant glow if it's polished with a little diesel oil, applied to a slightly damp cloth.

Windows

- Windows gleam when they're polished with a crumpled newspaper. The ink from the paper gives the glass a special shine.

- Spot spots on your windows – fast! Eliminate the guess-work of determining if streaks are on the inside or the outside of the glass. You'll always know if you wipe the outside vertically and the inside horizontally. Smudges and streaks will follow the direction in which you've rubbed.

- Clean windows and mirrors with very strong leftover tea. But leave the sugar out, please.

- Your window on the world will shine a little brighter if it's sponged clean with this solution. Combine ¼ cup corn-flour, 1 cup ammonia, and 1 cup white vinegar with 5 cups warm water. Towel off with newspaper or sponge mop.

- For the very best window cleaner ever, follow this recipe: combine ½ cup liquid household ammonia, 2 cups 70 per cent isopropyl rubbing alcohol, 1 tsp. washing-up liquid and enough water to make 16 cups of cleaner. Fill spray bottles and start squirting.

- Or try using ½ cup ammonia, ½ cup white vinegar, and 2 tbsp. cornflour. Shake well allow the suds to settle before starting to clean.

Window Blinds and Curtains

- Install your window blinds upside down for maximum privacy and light. Hook them to a bar in mid-window during the day, and to the top of the window frame at night.

2

- Rewind a floppy window blind by inserting the shaft end in a keyhole and turning the roller to tighten the spring.

- Window blinds won't flap in the breeze if you replace the pull ring with a small suction cup.

- Mend torn window blinds with a thin coating of colourless nail polish.

- Dust venetian blinds and shutter doors with oven-mitted hands. Quick and easy.

- Curtains won't tear as you thread them through a rod if you put the finger from an old glove on the tip of the rod.

- Curtain rings will slide more smoothly over wooden rods waxed with a candle or paraffin.

Furniture

- Your dust cloths will zip through the job if you give them a light spray of furniture polish, first.

- Cover scratches on dark wood furniture with brown felt pen ... OR ... brown shoe polish ... OR ... by rubbing a cut walnut onto the marks.

- To repair dents in wood furniture, swell the wood by pouring a small amount of hot water directly over the dent and allowing it to stand 5 min. If the gouge is severe, you may have to take more drastic action by spreading a clean, damp cloth over it, covering this with a dry cloth, and applying a warm iron to the surface of the wood.

- Stain unfinished furniture fast. Use a sponge rather than a brush.

- Want a super gloss on your table? Wax as usual, but buff with your power sander, wrapping it in several layers of flannelette, old nappies or a folded pillow case.

- Clean varnished woodwork with very strong leftover tea. The more the brew has steeped, the better this works.

- White rings will wipe off polished surfaces if you go over

2

the area with a soft cloth dampened with spirits of camphor.

- Remove most of the white ring from a polished mahogany table with this trick: Spread a thick coat of petroleum jelly over the stain and allow it to sit 48 hours. Then polish like mad and hope like hell!

- Make your own lemon oil furniture polish by adding 1 tbsp. lemon extract to 1 qt. liquid paraffin. Store in plastic spray bottles and wipe off furniture with a damp cloth.

- Mask scratches on white woodwork with white shoe-polish.

- Stop drawers from sticking by running a candle along the tops.

- Remove small surface scratches from glass-topped tables by lightly rubbing with toothpaste, rinsing, and then cleaning as normal.

- Reduce squeaks and corrosion of garden furniture with Vaseline which, unlike oil, will not stain slip covers. The cushions won't tear, by the way, if you wrap each spring under them with strapping tape.

- Help your piano stay in tune when the weather is hot and dry. Two uncapped jars of water placed away from the striking keys will help raise the humidity and keep your sound board from cracking. But be sure not to move the piano when the jars are there, and be sure they have flat, stable bottoms to help prevent spills.

Leather and Vinyl

- Leather furniture stays clean and supple if it's buffed with a monthly application of 2 parts linseed oil to 1 part white vinegar. Dry well.

- Revitalize tired leather chairs. Rub in the stiffly beaten white of an egg before polishing with a clean, dry cloth.

- Clean leather and vinyl upholstery with a squeeze of mild dishwashing detergent on a damp cloth.

■ Restore patent leather to its original beauty by rubbing lightly with Vaseline and polishing with a soft cloth ... OR ... buffing away finger prints with fresh, cold milk. Allow to dry before rubbing off.

Cane and Wicker

■ Wicker furniture won't become yellow and brittle if you scrub it with warm salt water when it needs cleaning.

■ A sagging cane chair will look like new if you rub a hot, wet sponge over the underneath of the cane. As the seat dries, it will shrink back to its original shape.

And Other Surfaces

■ Buff up your telephone with a cloth dampened with rubbing alcohol.

■ Clean and polish a gilt frame by carefully rubbing it with flat beer or the white of an egg. When that dries, buff with a clean, soft, dry cloth.

■ Dust silk and rayon lampshades with a soft baby's hairbrush you no longer need.

Give a Sparkle to your Bathroom

Tiles, Washbasins and Baths

- Banish soapy scum from the ceramic tiles around the bath. Sponge down with a solution of 1 gal. warm water, ¼ cup washing soda, ½ cup white vinegar, and ½ cup ammonia ... OR ... use full strength lemon juice, rinsing off with cold water.

- You can also remove the soapy film from tile grout and shower doors by wiping on and rinsing off full strength lemon juice.

- Whiten and clean discoloured tile grout. Apply a thick paste of bicarbonate of soda and water to the grouting, working in with an old toothbrush. Rinse well. A weak chlorine bleach solution works for slightly stained grout. And plain white toothpaste is a miracle cover-up if you're selling your house but don't have time to scrub that grotty grout.

- Remove stains from tile grout by rubbing with a circular typewriter eraser. The pumice in the eraser will scour the crevices and the brush on the other end will whisk away the dirt.

- Hard-water lime deposits will lift off toilet bowls allowed to soak an hour or more with 2 cups vinegar.

29

- Your soap dish won't be messy if you keep a folded face cloth in it or rest a nail brush in it, perching your soap on its bristles.

- Rub out washbasin and bathroom rust stains with a paste made from ½ cup hydrogen peroxide and 4 tbsp. cream of tartar, allowing to stand 5 min. or less, checking every minute to be sure this mixture will not etch the tub. Wipe off with a soft cloth; rinse thoroughly.

- Clean porcelain surfaces such as bathroom fixtures with a little cream of tartar on a damp cloth, or a little toothpaste. Both work if you've run short of regular cleanser.

- Whiten porcelain sinks by lining them with several layers of white paper towelling and pouring full strength bleach over it. Allow to rest undisturbed at least 30 min.

- Worn bathtub motifs will lift if you apply adhesive tape to them. Peel off the tape, and you'll peel off the motif, though you may need to apply a little contact cement solvent to get the last bits of glue off.

- Scrub your bath without bending. Wrap several thicknesses of nylon net over a child's toy broom, or use a cotton mop.

- Eliminate bathtub ring. Add bicarbonate of soda to the water.

The Loo

- Clean your toilet with a denture tablet. Allow to foam 5 min. before brushing and flushing.

30

■ Or pour some leftover cola into your toilet bowl, leaving it overnight. You won't believe the results.

Soap Savers

3

■ Soap slivers won't go to waste if you slice a deep pocket in the middle of a thick new bath sponge and tuck your bits of soap into it ... OR ... put them into a small drawstring bag sewn from an old washcloth. This makes a handy bath sponge.

■ Enjoy a bubble bath at no extra charge. Pop your soap slivers into a terry drawstring bag that you dangle from the tap at tub time, allowing the water to run over and through it.

■ You'll get a free cake of soap if you melt your odd bits over a double boiler and pour them into an oiled mould or travel soap container. When cool, turn out and allow to dry at least one month.

■ Soap will last a little longer if you remove it from its wrapping several days before using and allow it to dry out. Serve two purposes by keeping it in your lingerie drawer to lightly scent your undergarments.

■ Make your own soap flakes for handwashing lingerie. Simply grate those leftover pieces of old dried soap.

■ Save those slivers of soap! Stash them in a small mesh bag, rubbing this against your hands to chase away ground-in dirt.

■ Fill any squeeze bottle with shampoo. Those wide-necked bottles waste far too much shampoo – you'll control the flow better if you squeeze it rather than pour it out.

3

- To get a couple of extra uses from an aerosol shaving cream canister, run the container under hot water for a few seconds – not for too long or at a too hot temperature, though! Overheating could cause the can to explode.

- Save on bath oil by adding a dollop or two of Vaseline under the running tap.

And Some More Tidy Ideas

- No place to store those extra rolls of bargain toilet tissue? Slip them onto the handle of your bathroom plunger, hiding it under the sink.

- Keep the bottom of your bathroom waste basket clean. Line it with a paper plate.

- Revive an old sponge. Soak it in cold salted water overnight.

- Brushes and combs will come out like new if you occasionally soak them in a pot of lukewarm water to which 1 tbsp. bicarbonate of soda or a little ammonia has been added. Leave them in this solution 15 or 20 min.

- Trim a bathroom carpet to fit. Transfer a scale drawing of your room to a pattern cut from brown paper or newspaper. Lay the pattern over the rug before cutting.

- Remove grease marks from your hands by working in a few drops of undiluted liquid dish detergent.

- Your windows and bathroom mirrors won't steam up if they're cleaned as usual and then wiped with a glycerine-dampened cloth.

Laundry Made Simple

Keeping Whites White

- Clothes yellowed by chlorine bleach will be snowy white once more if they're soaked several hours in a solution of 1 part white vinegar to 12 parts cold water.

- Cottons will stay sparkling white if they're briefly boiled in a pot of water with a few drops of ammonia or half a cut lemon.

- White nylon fabrics won't yellow if they're soaked in bicarbonate of soda and water before laundering.

... and Coloureds Bright

- Coloured fabrics are less likely to run in wash water to which a few tablespoons of salt or ½ cup epsom salts have been added.

- Fluff won't cling to dark colours in the wash if you add ½ cup white vinegar to the final rinse cycle.

- Dark socks won't attract fluff if they're washed in a knotted pair of tights.

Looking after Your Table Linen

- Table napkins are less effort to iron if you dampen every third one, placing it between two dry serviettes, sandwich style, and rolling them up for an hour or so until you're ready to press them.

- Press napkins and hankies without an iron. Lay them flat, under a couple of very heavy books.

4

- Remove candlewax from your tablecloth by ironing the waxy stain between two pieces of an unwaxed brown paper bag.

- Damask tablecloths won't yellow between uses if they are stored tightly wrapped in a dark plastic rubbish bag. This keeps out light and air, and saves a second washing . . . OR . . . store the cloth folded inside out. When you need it, the yellow stains will be on its underside.

Dealing with Delicate Items

- Delicate items won't stretch and tangle in your washing machine's spin cycle if you drop them into a pillowcase first.

- Clothes that must be laundered individually won't wear out as quickly if you add a couple of towels to the wash and dry cycles.

- Tights will last longer without runs if you wet them well, squeeze them out, and store them in a plastic bag in the freezer overnight. Hang up to dry and then wear as normal.

- Save money cleaning silk garments. If you're very careful, most silks can be hand-washed even though dry cleaning is recommended. Use lukewarm water and a protein hair shampoo, rinsing several times with a few drops of white vinegar added to the rinse water. Always dry away from sunlight, and never sprinkle before ironing. Iron with a warm – not hot! – setting, on the wrong side only, placing a clean cloth between the iron and the silk.

Ways with Woollens

- Hand-washed wool sweaters won't itch if you add a table-spoon of castor oil to the final rinse water.

- Don't throw out that shrunken sweater. You may be able to stretch it by dissolving 1 oz. borax in a small amount of hot water and mixing in 1 gal. tepid water. Immerse garment in this solution and pull gently into shape, rinsing in 1 gal. of tepid water to which 2 tbsp. white vinegar have been added. Roll in towel to remove excess moisture; dry flat.

Iron out Your Problems

■ Speedy ironers will love this hint – why spend more time on that dreary chore than you have to? Flip any garment with buttons upside down, resting the buttons on a soft terry towel. Then iron away – zip, zip – no worries about buttons popping off, and no fussing.

■ No sleeve board on your ironing board? Keep an empty cardboard roll handy or wrap a clean dish towel around a rolling pin. You'll be able to open seams flat without creasing the sleeve. Do take the garment off, first ...

■ De-coke your iron and it will glide smoothly again. Simply sprinkle table salt on wax paper and iron directly over it.

■ If you can't iron dampened clothes right away, stash them in the fridge, so mildew won't develop.

■ Save a few minutes when it's time to change the sheets. You won't have to hunt for matching sets if you put the fixings for each bed together as a "pack." Grab a pack as you need one and be on your way.

35

And Don't Forget

■ Get all the soap out of your wash by adding ½ cup of vinegar to the rinse cycle.

■ Clothes won't blow off their hangers on an outdoor line if you anchor them with a clothes peg. Clip the pin to your line, and you're in business . . . OR . . . anchor each hanger with a twist tie . . . OR . . . use two hangers rather than one, reversing them so the hooks form a circle.

■ An easy way to avoid clogged wash basin drains is to snap an old nylon stocking to the end of the rinse hose. As the machine empties into the basin, an astounding amount of fluff and other debris will be trapped by this homemade filter. Think of the plumbing costs you'll save!

■ Give your washing machine a thorough cleaning now and then by adding two cups of white vinegar to a normal warm water cycle, with the machine otherwise empty. This clears away clogs and soap scum.

■ Drip dry several tea towels at one time by clipping onto a skirt hanger.

■ Flat bedsheets will stay put if you tie a knot at each bottom corner, tucking each under the mattress.

■ Freshly changed beds will smell inviting (to those who aren't allergy-prone) if you sprinkle the finest dusting of baby powder on the mattress before smoothing on clean sheets. Cosy!

Food, Glorious Food

Meat and Fish

- Leftover beef stew can be blenderized to a puree and used as a base for Scotch broth and other soups.

- Stretch a pound of mince by making spaghetti sauce on day one, adding kidney beans and spices to the leftover sauce on day two, serving as chili, and pouring the leftover chili, cooked rice or potatoes, and a few diced mixed vegetables into a crust for meat pie on day three.

- Extend chuck steaks or roasts by sectioning them into quarters. Mince the first portion for meatballs or patties, dice the next for stew, cut the third into shish kebab or slices served in sweet and sour sauce, and cook the remaining as pot roast. Toss all bones into the soup pot.

- Cutting your own chicken and chops from whole fryers and loins will easily save 30 to 50 per cent on your meat bill.

- Stuffing poultry is a snap if you put the dressing into a well-greased cheese cloth before packing it into the cavity. You'll get every smidgen out.

- Discount meat bargains are most often found in your supermarket at closing time Saturday night.

- Your hamburgers will be juicier if you add a grated raw potato to each pound of meat ... OR ... add ¼ cup cold water.

- Two eggs are the nutritional equivalent of a three-ounce serving of meat. Substitute them for a change of pace.

5

- Tenderize tough meat by marinating overnight in ½ cup white vinegar and 1 cup beef broth. Rub steaks with equal parts of oil and vinegar and allow to marinate 30 min., pricking with a fork. Soak stewing fowl in full strength vinegar for several hours before cooking, and you'll never know it was a bargain bird.

- Cook tough meat in tea. Tannin is a tenderizer and you won't notice its flavour in stew.

- Separate home-made hamburgers bound for the freezer with the wax paper liners from old cereal boxes, cut to size. Nice and thick, they peel off the frozen patties without ripping.

- Dice bacon quickly by trimming the ends of several slices in the packet.

- No salmon or tuna for your fish casserole? Substitute canned mackerel and save money. And you can make your own fishcakes by combining a medium-sized can of mackerel, one egg, a little chopped onion, and a generous dollop or two of leftover mashed potatoes.

- Poach fish the easy way – in your dishwasher! Extra large fish – even those too big for your oven – will come out moist and tender. Double wrap in heavy duty foil, seasoning inside and out with lemon, pepper, seasoning salt, onion salt, a light dash of garlic salt, chopped celery, and butter. Top fish with fresh lemon slices for extra zip. Very large fish may require two full cycles, including the drying cycle. Make sure your water is very hot, or the fish will not cook properly.

Soup

- Skim the fat from soups and stews by running a few cheesecloth-wrapped ice cubes over the surface. The fat clings to the cloth.

- Making soup stock is always convenient if you pop celery heels, carrot tops, and other raw vegetable scraps into a plastic bag in the freezer each time you cook.

- Dried vegetables make excellent additions to soups and stews. Dry mushrooms, pepper, carrot, and green onion slices the easy way – by placing them on a flat plate above the stove top vent.

- Thicken soup with a finely grated potato or instant potato flakes.

- Tone down oversalted soups and stews by adding 1 tsp. sugar and 1 tsp. vinegar, cooking a little longer ... OR ... by adding a few chunks of raw potato. The potato absorbs the excess salt; remove it after cooking.

5

Salad

- Tomatoes and cucumbers taste best when stored at room temperature.

- Celery will keep for weeks if it's stored in a wide-mouthed jar or coffee can filled with cold water.

- Cream cheese decorations won't slide off salad if you scrape the salad surface lightly with the piping tube before applying your designs.

- Wilted lettuce leaves make excellent casings for baking fish; the fish will remain moist as it cooks. They are also ideal for keeping poultry moist as it roasts or bakes. Slightly wilted leaves can be chopped and added to soups or stews.

- Lettuce will not go rusty if you remove its core. Bang the lettuce head hard on the kitchen counter – the core should twist right out.

- Lettuce keeps longer stored in a brown paper bag or on a paper towel in the produce drawer of your fridge.

- Revive wilted lettuce by quickly plunging it into hot water and then into ice water to which a few drops of cider vinegar have been added.

- Lettuce will perk up if you let it sit in a bowl of ice water containing a few sliced potatoes.

- Making salad for a crowd? Spin your lettuce dry in the washing machine. A few seconds in a well-sealed clean pillowcase does the trick.

Vegetables

- Make your steamer do double duty by cooking potatoes in the bottom of your pot while a steamed vegetable cooks on top.

- Peel thick broccoli and asparagus stems, cooking them along with the more tender parts.

- Remove the strings from cooked, mashed pumpkin by whipping with an electric mixer – the strings will wrap themselves around the beaters.

- Canned asparagus tips won't snap off if you open the tin at the bottom rather than at the top.

- Cook fresh asparagus upright in a coffee perc with the lid on.

- Too much liquid in your mashed potatoes? Add a little skimmed milk powder.

- Enhance the flavour of fresh corn by adding a little sugar and a few of the inner green husks to the cooking water.

- Remove every smidgen of silk from a corn cob with a few swift downward strokes of a dampened paper towel.

- Vegetables cooked in broth develop a nice flavour.

- The unused portion of an onion stores longer in the fridge if it's still wearing the skin.

- Don't buy onions that have sprouted green tops – that's a sign that at least one layer has gone bad.

- Buy onions by the sack each Autumn, hanging the bag in a dark, cool place. It's much cheaper than buying them each time you shop, and you'll be less likely to run out.

- To keep onions from sprouting, wrap each in aluminium foil.

- Onions won't make you weep if you peel them under cold water ... OR ... refrigerate them first.

- A small tin of tomato paste is an economical substitute for the large tin of tomatoes called for in many recipes. Just use less seasoning with the paste and more liquid.

- Freeze leftover tomato paste in ice cube trays, repackaging in small freezer bags to use as needed.

- Boiled potatoes will not darken if you add 1 tbsp. vinegar to the cooking water.

Pickles

- No cheesecloth to hold pickling spices? Use a stainless metal tea infuser or the snipped leg of a clean pair of discarded tights.

- Pickle beetroot inexpensively by boiling them in a mixture of pickle juice and a little sugar and allowing them to sit overnight.

5

- Scrub dill cucumbers with a minimum of fuss. Wash them for a minute or two in your clothes washer, using a gentle cycle and cold water.

- Leftover pickle juice can be used several ways. Thin mayonnaise with it for coleslaw dressing: marinate onion slices in it for 24 hours before serving as a side dish; use it to pickle leftover cooked beetroot; give French dressing extra zip by adding a few tablespoons of it.

- No garlic cloves? Use ⅛ tsp. garlic powder, instead.

Fruit

- Cut lemons won't go to waste if you squeeze the remaining juice and freeze and store it in ice cube trays.

- Freeze lemon skins for future use. These grate well and a little can be trimmed off for flavour as required. Freeze and store lemon, grapefruit, and orange skins until you have enough for lemonade.

- Lemons will stay fresh longer if you store them in a bowl of cold water in the fridge. They'll keep up to three months this way.

- To peel the white pith from oranges without too much effort, pour boiling water over the fruit and allow to stand 5 min. before removing the skin.

- To get just a few drops of juice from a lemon you don't wish to cut right away, puncture with a toothpick or fork and gently squeeze in that spot.

- Citrus fruits will yield more juice if you roll them gently on a counter top or soak them in warm water for 15 min. before squeezing.

- Orange and lemon peel is best whisked from your grater with a pastry brush.

- Make your own economical orange drink. Whip in blender until frothy: 1 egg, 1 cup fresh orange juice, ½ cup skimmed milk powder, 2 tbsp. sugar, ¼ tsp. vanilla, and ½ cup crushed ice. Serves three generously.

- A dry lemon will yield juice if you soak it in boiling water and allow to stand 5 min. before cooling.

- Berry picking is far easier if you string two coffee cans around your neck, letting them dangle near your midriff. Saves stooping and really speeds the job.

- Save your hands during fruit preserving season by wearing surgical gloves as you work.

- Make fruit jellies in winter by freezing summer's pureed berry juice bounty in plastic ice cream containers until ready to use.

- Seals will lift off homemade jams and jellies far more easily if you lay a small piece of string across the neck of the jar before putting the seal on. A quick yank on both ends will remove the top when you're ready to use the jam.

- Make your own delicious pancake sauce from fresh local berries. Blenderize or puree the fruit, straining to remove the pulp and seeds, and add an equal volume of sugar to the remaining juice. Boil until sugar is dissolved; bottle and refrigerate.

- Make an economical jelly at a fraction the cost of the name brand product by combining fruit syrup, unflavoured gelatine powder, and a little colouring.

Bread

- Leave homemade yeast bread and bun dough to prove in the dishwasher – the humid heat left after a load of dishes will work wonders.

- Greased bread dough won't stick or dry out if you allow it to rise in a large plastic bag.

- Make your own croutons for pennies. Saute 1 cup soft cubed bread crumbs in 3 tbsp. butter, stirring in a mixture of ¼ tsp. basil, ¼ tsp. oregano, and ½ tsp. seasoned salt.

Pastry

- Sliced biscuits from refrigerated dough will always be perfectly shaped if you freeze the dough in small frozen juice cans, slicing it as it thaws.

- Pastry won't break as you ease it into the pan if you fold it loosely over your rolling pin as you transfer it from your pastry board.

- Pastry will be flakier if you include 1 tbsp. orange or lemon juice as part of the liquid.

- No shortening for your pie crust? Substitute an equal amount of peanut butter.

Butter and Cheese

- Make your own herb butter and everyone you know will ask for the recipe. This one's extra good. Whip ½ cup butter until creamy, beating in 2 tbsp. finely chopped onion, 2 cloves minced or crushed garlic, 2 tsp. poppy seeds, 2 tsp. sesame seeds, ¾ tsp. dill seeds, and ¾ tsp. caraway seeds. Spread on slices of bread and heat on baking sheet about 8 min. in 350 degree F. oven, or until butter melts and bread is hot right through. This is also terrific when spread on light toast and quickly heated until golden.

- Soften margarine or butter quickly by covering with a heated bowl.

- Make your own whipped butter and save money by doubling the volume of butter on hand. Whip 1 lb. butter or margarine until soft and fluffy, slowly adding ½ cup cold water, ½ cup oil, and a dash of salt. Beat until completely mixed and store in the fridge. This will remain soft even at cold temperatures.

- If a recipe calls for sharp cheddar cheese and you have mild cheese only, add a dash of pepper, dry mustard, and Worcestershire sauce to your grated cheese. That will sharpen it up.

5

■ Slice cheese thin enough for rapid melting by using a potato peeler if you haven't a cheese slice. Cheese sliced this way is also a convenient serving size for toddlers who'd like a taste without waste.

Eggs

■ Boiled eggs won't crack if you punch a small hole in the wide end before plunging them into water. A sewing needle inserted through a wine cork works well for this job.

■ Hard-boiled eggs won't ooze all over the pan as they cook if you make sure the water in the pan is cold when you start. Bring to the boil, turn off and wait 20 min. before running under cold water to chill.

■ A quick way to crack hard-boiled eggs prior to peeling is to shake them in the pan in which they were cooked. The finely shattered shells will lift off in large chunks, leaving the egg undamaged.

■ Scooping up a broken egg is easier if you sprinkle it with salt and allow it to set first. Then pick it up with a damp paper towel.

■ No eggs in the house? You can substitute 2 tbsp. vinegar mixed with 1 tsp. bicarbonate of soda for the missing egg in most recipes. But don't try this for more than one missing egg.

Milk

■ No milk for your pancakes? Substitute soda water and they will practically float away. But use up all the batter. It won't keep.

■ Make your own sweetened condensed milk and save a small fortune. This makes 12 oz. and can be used in any recipe calling for this type of milk, but must be stored in the fridge for 24 hours before using, to develop the flavour. Do not store more than one week in the fridge. Mix in blender about one minute or until sugar has partially dissolved: ¼ cup hot water and ¾ cup granulated sugar. While continuing to blend, slowly add 1¼ cups powdered milk. Cover and refrigerate. No one will know the difference!

■ Milk powder will slice your milk bill in half. If the kids rebel against drinking it, they'll never notice it in your cooking.

■ Milk and cream won't stick to the pan in which they're scalded if you rinse it with cold water before and after use.

■ No buttermilk or sour milk? Just add 1 tsp. lemon juice or ½ tsp. bicarbonate of soda to each cup of milk the recipe calls for.

■ No coffee cream? Substitute powdered milk thickening it with fresh milk. But use less liquid than you would if you were reconstituting it with water.

■ No whipping cream? Add a well-mashed banana to one stiffly beaten egg white, adding sugar to taste. This is especially delicious on banana cream pie.

Seasonings and Dressings

■ Make your own seasoning by finely chopping small amounts of parsley, green onions, carrots, celery, and parsnips, adding one part salt to four parts vegetables. Mix well and spread on a baking sheet to dry. Should stay fresh about a year.

■ Make your own flavoured vinegar by adding dill or celery seeds, tarragon, or rosemary to white vinegar brought just to simmering and stored, tightly capped, in the fridge.

■ Spices will keep longer in a cool, dark place – a spice rack just over the oven is the worst possible place.

■ Paprika, cayenne, chili, and curry powder will last longer and keep their flavour better if they're stored in the fridge.

■ No vinegar in the house? You can substitute grapefruit juice for the vinegar in many salad dressings.

46

Barbecues

■ Dripping fat won't mess your barbecue coals as you rotisserie meat if you cut an old coffee tin lengthwise, crimping the two halves together end to end ... OR ... make a simple drip pan from heavy duty foil.

■ Recycle used charcoal pieces by transferring the still-hot coals to an old pressure cooker with a tight-fitting lid and safety valve. With their air supply gone, the coals will be snuffed out immediately, and can be re-used up to four times. The valve on the pressure cooker allows the build-up of warm air to escape, preventing a possible explosion. This really saves money during barbecue season.

■ Here's the lazy man's way to clean barbecue grills: Cover the grill completely with heavy duty foil, shiny side in, and place over hot coals. Remove foil after 10 min. and the dirt should drop right off ... OR ... if your bath needs scrubbing anyway, allow to soak in the tub with enough hot water to cover, with ½ cup ammonia to cut the grease.

■ Barbecue racks will stay cleaner if you paint or spray them with vegetable oil before grilling your meat.

■ Picnickers: You'll never forget the salt and pepper if you mix three parts salt to one part pepper, keeping this in an empty film canister tucked into your picnic basket.

■ Your picnic tablecloth will stay put in the strongest breeze if you snap each corner tight against the table with four clothes pegs kept in your basket for just that purpose.

■ Cottage cheese containers make dandy picnic boxes.

■ A simple emergency frying pan can be fashioned from a bent clothes hanger and a foil pie plate or doubled-over length of foil.

■ Deflect the heat of a camp fire from your hand as you cook sausages or marshmallows by threading a foil pie plate over a straightened coat hanger grilling those foods over the fire.

■ Ever tried to make a "buddy burner"? It's a great emergency camp stove. Cut a flap at the top of a large washed-out beer or coffee tin, crimping the edges flat for safety. Turn the flap down and to the inside. Flip the tin over – its base becomes the top of your stove. Now your fuel: wrap a strip of corrugated cardboard tightly inside a small washed-out tuna fish tin, with one end removed. Push a birthday candle in the centre, dribbling paraffin wax over all. The small tin goes inside the flap of the larger tin. Punch two holes on each top side of the larger tin, just below your cooking surface, for ventilation.

Waste Note – Want Not

■ Leftovers will be plan-overs if you methodically section them into TV dinner trays and freeze for a quickie dinner one future night when you haven't time to cook.

■ Dried cakes will become moist and tender if you store them for a few days in an airtight container with a slice or two of fresh bread.

■ Stale biscuits can be crushed with a rolling pin (put them in a plastic bag and you won't have a mess) and used to make flan bases. A food processor or blender, of course, saves time for this job and others like it.

■ Recrisp nuts, crackers, biscuits and potato chips by spreading them on a baking sheet and heating for about ten minutes at 250° F.

■ Get every drop of ketchup from the jar by swishing it out with some of the liquid called for in your recipe.

■ Stop pimentos from spoiling by freezing the leftovers, breaking off frozen bits as needed ... OR ... by covering with a thin layer of oil before replacing in the fridge.

■ Chopped onion freezes well. Don't just let it linger in the fridge and spoil.

■ Yeast will keep indefinitely if you freeze the unopened package. Opened packages stay potent about three months.

5

- Soften hardened brown sugar by adding a slice of apple to the bag or canister in which it's stored. A very fresh slice of white bread will also soften it.

- Coffee will keep longer if it's stored in the fridge or freezer.

- Tea, however, is best stored at room temperature.

- Make your ground coffee go further. Mix 2 heaped tbsp. ground chicory with 1 lb. coffee, and then measure just one-half to two-thirds the amount you would normally use.

- Paper coffee filters can be re-used up to six times. Just rinse them out and let them dry in the filter cone.

- Save money when you mash potatoes! Whip them with ½-to-1 cup powdered milk and the potato cooking water instead of using fresh milk.

- Make your own economical hot chocolate powder just like the kind you buy in the store. Mix 8 cups skimmed milk powder, 1 cup cocoa, and 2 cups granulated sugar in a large bowl, combining 1 cup at a time in the blender for a finely-powdered lump-free mixture. Store in an airtight container. Use 1½ tbsp. per cup, blending with a little evaporated milk and adding boiling water.

- Freshen stale tobacco with a slice of raw apple or potato.

Improvising on Utensils

- Separate eggs effortlessly by plopping into a kitchen funnel. The yolk will be trapped as the white drops through.

- Need an extra pastry roller for an extra pair of helping hands? Use a wine bottle.

- If you're caught without a corkscrew, you can sometimes force a cork from a bottle by running very hot water over the neck.

Sticky Problems

5

- Separate bacon slices from the rest of the package by first rolling the package forward, then back on itself.

- Cutting marshmallows is simpler if you dip your scissors into icing sugar or water first ... one or the other, not both!

- Spaghetti won't stick if you add a drop of oil to the cooking water.

- Plastic wrap won't cling to itself if you store it in the fridge.

- Salt shakers will pour freely if you keep a few grains of rice inside them.

- Mixing bowls will hold steady if you rest them on a damp cloth while you're mixing.

- Your batter won't splatter if you poke aluminium foil over your beater rods, tucking it over the edge of the bowl. The foil will trap wayward splotches.

- Rice will cook lighter and fluffier if you add 1 tbsp. lemon juice to the cooking water.

- The top of your fruit cakes will not burn if you reserve a little plain batter before you add the fruit. Pour this unfruited batter over the top of the cake before you start to bake, and the fruit underneath won't be overdone.

- You can also stop a cake from browning too fast if you put a pan of water on the top rack. The cake will bake right through without scorching.

- No baking powder in your cupboard? For each cup of flour your recipe calls for, substitute 2 tsp. cream of tartar, 1 tsp. bicarbonate of soda, and ½ tsp. salt for the baking powder you don't have.

- To test the freshness of old baking powder, add a teaspoonful to a cup of hot water. If it bubbles furiously, it's fine. If not, buy a fresh box.

- No whole wheat flour? Make some. Combine 5¼ cups white flour, ¾ cup wheat germ, and 1½ cups natural bran. For a finer texture, buzz the bran in your blender, first.

- No icing sugar? Pulverize granulated sugar in your blender.

- No semi-sweet chocolate squares on hand? Substitute 1 oz. unsweetened chocolate with 5 tsp. added sugar for every 2 oz. semi-sweet you need.

Quell that Smell!

- Kill onion or garlic smells on hands and cutting boards by rubbing a cut lemon or a cloth dampened with vinegar over the area.

- Garlic smells won't linger on your fingers if you pound the cloves between two pieces of waxed paper.

- Cooking odours will vanish if you boil 1 tsp. ground cloves or cinnamon in 2 cups water for about 10 min. in an uncovered saucepan on the stove.

- Cabbage and onions won't smell so strong while they're cooking if you simmer a small pot of vinegar on the stove.

- Fish, onion, and other strong food odours will disappear if you wipe hands, cooking utensils, and cutting boards with full-strength vinegar and then rinse with soapy water.

- Remove odours from jars and bottles by soaking several hours in a solution of warm water and dry mustard powder.

- Deodorize your fridge by placing a small paper cupful of activated charcoal on the bottom rack ... OR ... a small cupful of bicarbonate of soda.

- Clear cigarette smoke from a room by lighting a candle.

- Smoke-scented clothes will smell fresh again if you hang them on the shower rod or bathroom door, fill the bath with hot water, and add a medium-sized bottle of vinegar to it. The vinegar in the steam will clear away the odour of smoke.

- Ashtrays will smell clean again if you scour them with a little bicarbonate of soda.

- Deodorize your rug by sprinkling with bicarbonate of soda and allowing to stand 15 or 20 min. before vacuuming.

- Freshen musty cupboards by hanging up a tea infuser full of damp used coffee grounds for several hours or overnight.

Do-it-yourself

Painters' Pointers

- Remembering exact paint shades is an easy trick if you dip a lolly stick into the paint and take it with you as you hunt for curtains and rugs.

- You'll never forget the paint and wallpaper codes for each room if you jot the information on the top of the door to the room.

- Here's a fast-drying putty: Fill the holes to be patched with a thick paste of cornflour mixed with some of the paint you're using.

- Painting window frames is easier if you stick strips of wet newspaper to the glass – no need to scrape away paint slop-overs.

- The quickest way to paint wrought-iron railings is to dip a small sponge in the paint and rub it over the rails, wearing gloves as you work. A paint brush is too slow for this fussy job.

- Clean paint-stained hands with a little margarine if you're out of turpentine or paint thinner.

- Strain paint through an old pair of tights.

- You'll always know how much paint is left in the tin if you wrap a rubber band around it as you seal it, marking the remaining level.

- Store opened paint upside down – the film will form on the bottom, not the top.

- Paint won't form a scum if you rest a foil pie-plate lightly on the surface.

6

- Stop drips as you paint the ceiling by poking a foil pudding basin through the handle of your brush, resting it just under the bristles.

- Protect your glasses from paint splatters by covering the lenses with clear plastic fastened with elastic bands.

- No need to wash paint brushes every time you're called from the job. Pop them into plastic bags and tuck into the freezer: allow about an hour to thaw before painting again.

- Protect your hanging light fixture or chandelier from splatters as you paint by covering it with a large plastic rubbish bag or one of the filmy see-through bags from your dry cleaner.

- Protect the knob of a door you're painting by taping a plastic bag over it.

- Clean hardened, caked-on paint brushes by simmering in hot vinegar until softened, then washing in hot soapy water.

- The best way to pick dried paint from old brushes is to run an old comb through the bristles.

- Oil-based paint stains will wash off clothes pre-treated with equal parts of ammonia and turpentine.

- Strain paint without straining yourself. Cut an old piece of wire mesh in a circle slightly smaller than the diameter of your paint can, dropping it into the open can. As it sinks to the bottom, so will the lumps.

- Paint smells vanish if you leave a large bucket or bowl of water or a freshly cut onion in the room overnight. And farm dwellers swear by a handful of hay, immersed in a bucket of water in the freshly painted room.

- A freshly painted cupboard will be fragrant for months if you add a few drops of perfume to the paint.

- Paint cans won't drip if you pop a paper plate underneath.

54

- Protect windows from splatters while you paint the frames. Coat each pane with laundry soap or spray it with a non-foamy cleanser that will wash off when the frames are dry. Abutting strips of wet newspaper against the frames also saves the glass.

- Protect your shoes as you paint. Slip each into a plastic bag, securing at the ankle with a rubber band. Old socks work, too. And never mind if the neighbours think you've slipped your moorings.

- Paint touch-ups are less bother if you keep a little extra of each colour in a clean, empty nail polish bottle.

- Want to know if your new drywall is ready to paint? Tack a piece of plastic wrap to the wall using masking tape, and leave on at least one day. If moisture forms inside the wrap, wait a little longer before painting.

- To paint or not to paint . . . that is the question. Don't even consider outdoor paint jobs in the very hot summer or during winter's grip. Don't paint if it looks like rain, and don't paint for at least one day after a heavy rainfall. Don't paint too early in the day, either, while the dew is on the grass. And surely there must be other excuses, too.

- Your ladder won't leave annoying marks as you paint the outside of your house if you paint the top few inches of the ladder in the same colour as the job. Slipping an old pair of heavy wool socks over the top of the ladder also saves the walls.

- To remove mildew from painted surfaces, combine 5 cups water with 4 cups chlorine bleach, 1 oz. laundry detergent, and 3 oz. TSP or trisodium phosphate.

- Worn-out transfers can often be lifted from painted surfaces such as cots and dressers by pressing sticky sellotape against them.

- White paint will become even whiter if you add a few drops of black paint to it.

- Paint every other step on a well-travelled staircase, marking the path to follow with paper. When the painted steps are dry, reverse the procedure.

Wallpapering Winners

- Loosen old wallpaper to be peeled off with equal parts of vinegar and hot water, liberally applied with a paint roller.

- Wallpaper goes up easier and stays on longer if you add a pinch of alum and a pinch of salt to the paste.

- Burst those wallpaper bubbles. Simply use a pin, pressing the area flat with your finger.

- Wallpaper seams stay put if each gets a good rolling with a chair caster.

- A neat trick to protect wallpaper when you're hanging pictures: cut a small "V" in the spot where you want to drive your nail, gently peeling back the paper. Hang the picture – but when you decide it's time to rearrange the room and you'd like the picture somewhere else, glue the paper back over the spot where you drove the nail.

- Perk up soiled wallpaper by rubbing with a clean cloth dipped in dry powdered borax, and then going over the area with a second clean cloth.

- Remove greasy stains on wallpaper. Lay a clean blotter over the marks, applying a warm iron to the soiled spots.

- To stop greasy stains from bleeding onto new wallpaper when you haven't removed the old paper underneath, coat the stains with shellac, first.

Tackling Nuts, Bolts and Screws

- Aerosol can lids make excellent workshop holders for nuts and bolts.

- Not sure which way to twist that bolt? Remind yourself that right is tight and left is loose.

- Tighten a wiggly screw by enlarging it rather then by trying to make the hole smaller. Wrap sellotape around its threads or coat it with clear nail polish, allowing the polish to dry before you reinsert the screw.

- Another method is to strip the insulating cover from a spare piece of electrical wiring, allowing the plastic to grip the screw as you wind it round the threads, or to jam the wooden end of a matchstick into the hole.

- Loosen rusted nuts and bolts with a few drops of ammonia ... OR ... by swabbing with a cotton ball dipped in Coca-Cola ... OR ... by soaking several minutes in a few drops of peroxide.

- Loosen rusty screws by pouring a few drops of iodine or vinegar on them.

- Stubborn bottle tops will usually twirl off with the aid of a nutcracker.

And Hammer and Nails

- Nails are less likely to split wood if they're blunted before driving.

- Nails are less likely to crack or chip plaster if they're warmed before driving.

- Nailing in cramped quarters? Tape the head of your nail to the hammer – that way, you won't get frustrated trying to hold it.

- Hold small nails and tacks for hammering between the teeth of an old comb ... OR ... gripped in a pair of tweezers ... OR ... by nailing through very thin cardboard.

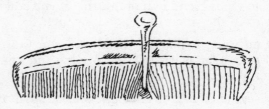

- Need a mallet? Slip a rubber crutch tip over the head of your hammer.

- Drive a picture hanger without cracking the plaster by first placing a small strip of Sellotape on the spot.

Door Troubles Solved

- Silence squeaky door hinges by running a lead pencil over them several times ... OR ... by giving them a quick wipe with a little vaseline ... OR ... by rubbing with a cake of soap ... OR ... by spraying with vegetable oil.

- You'll know exactly where a door is sticking if you line the frame with carbon paper. The paper will mark those spots where the fit is too snug.

- Doors will open and shut more easily and with less sticking if you grease the top, bottom, and sides with a few drops of liquid paraffin.

- Find air leaks around doors and windows just a little faster – light a match and watch where the smoke goes.

Small Repairs

- Here's a clever way to eliminate blisters from wood veneer. Using a hypodermic needle, inject a small amount of glue under the wood. Press flat until set.

- Repair pinholes in your doors and window screens. A dab of clear nail polish or colourless glue does the job. Repeat until the hole is patched, allowing to dry between applications.

- Wood patch jobs blend in more readily if you add a little sawdust from the wood to the glue or filler.

- Here's a nifty way to patch a small hole in the wall. Drive in a golf tee, as far as it will go, trimming and sanding it flat. Then plaster and paint.

- Repair a scratched mirror like new. Shellac a flat piece of foil over the scratch, and tell yourself you're beautiful.

Rust Busters

- The threads of outdoor light bulbs won't corrode if you coat them lightly with vaseline.

- Exposed outdoor locks won't rust if you wrap them in a plastic sandwich bag, securing it with a rubber band.

- Scissor blades won't rust if they're regularly rubbed with crumpled wax paper. Snip the paper into shreds and you'll keep the edge of each blade rust-free, too.

6

Steps and Ladders

- Your ladder won't sink into soft earth if you place each of its feet into an empty coffee can.

- Stepladders are less slippery with a strip of sandpaper glued to each step.

- You won't knock your shins on a stepladder if you glue draught excluder to the front of each step.

- Ladders won't scratch your walls if you drape an old pair of workgloves over the tops.

- Steady the bottom of a ladder by slipping each foot into an old rubber galosh.

Cupboards and Basements

- Utilize that space under the hall stairs. Plumbed and vented, this makes a dandy spot for a washer and dryer, hidden behind bifold doors.

- Convert a seldom-used clothes cupboard to a small study. Take off the door, building in a desk and shelves.

■ Want to find out why your basement is damp? A mirror taped to a basement wall tells the story. If the moisture is caused by seepage, the mirror remains unchanged. If condensation is the cause, the mirror will cloud up.

Bulbs and Batteries

■ Unscrewing and replacing out-of-reach lightbulbs is simpler if you tape the suction cup from a child's bow and arrow to the end of a broom handle and use this for grasping the bulb.

■ Remove the base of a broken lightbulb from its socket by inserting the handle of a rubber-coated screwdriver into it and twisting ... OR ... by pushing a wine cork into the base and twisting.

■ Dry cell batteries will have a longer shelf life if you store them in airtight plastic bags in the deep freeze. But ... let them thaw 24 hours before using.

Other Smart Ideas

■ You'll know at a glance what's inside each workshop container if you tape a sample of the contents to the outside.

■ Thin thickened glue with a little rubbing alcohol.

■ Most hardened glues will loosen with hot vinegar.

■ Even pitch and gum deposits will wipe off your circular saw blades if you apply oven cleaner and let stand a few minutes before rubbing.

■ Applying glue to large areas is easier if you use a cheap paint roller rather than a brush.

■ Greasy hands should come clean with neat washing up liquid ... OR ... use a spoonful of sugar.

■ If you need extra light but haven't got a free hand as you work, tape a torch to the inside of your forearm.

■ Need a third hand as you solder? Hold the object to be

6

soldered in the grip of a mousetrap. A clothes peg will also hold both ends of any soldering job in place.

- You've always got a measuring tape in your pocket if you remember that a pound note is 133mm long and 65mm wide.

- Improvise when your small electric motor needs a new replacement brush. The carbon electrode in the core of D-size dry cell batteries can be adapted to this use and sanded down to fit.

- Nylon and polypropelene cords won't fray if you melt the cut ends for a few seconds under a match.

- Straighten a slightly bent small drill by rolling it between two blocks of wood. This doesn't always work, but it's worth a try.

- Sharpen scissors quickly and simply by cutting medium grade sandpaper with them.

- Steel wool won't scratch your hands if you hold it in half a tennis ball.

- Dissolve dry putty blobs with a little household ammonia.

- Bend aluminium tubing without kinking it. Fill it with sand, first, plugging both ends.

- Lay bricks like a pro. A ⅜ inch dowel makes a perfect spacer, and will keep your bricks straight.

- Workshop razor blades can be stored safely if they're imbedded in a small block of Styrofoam. No cut fingers, no searching through your box of odds and ends. And ...

- Double-edged razor blades won't nick your fingers if you protect one edge with the stapled end of a match-book, or a couple of thicknesses of masking tape.

6

6

- Hold those tubes of contact cement and model glue neatly in your workshop. Fasten each to a bulldog clip, hanging it above your work bench.

- Store your drill in a holster made from a cut plastic squash container. Bolt it to your workshop wall.

- Make less mess when you're drilling. Fasten a sheet of paper under the spot where you're working, taping up the bottom third to form a catch-all basket. Neat and nifty.

- Fiddly sanding jobs are easier if you use an emery board or glue sandpaper to both sides of an ice lolly stick.

- Make your own scouring pad by dipping a square of leftover carpet in bicarbonate of soda. This works well on saw blades.

Stain Removing

Stain Removing

- Biro . . . Squirt with hairspray or rub with a dab of toothpaste before laundering.

- Biro . . . wash Biro ink marks off leather or vinyl by rubbing gently with milk. This isn't foolproof, but often does the trick.

- Blood . . . Sprinkle the stain with unseasoned meat tenderizer or salt, dampening slightly. Allow to work 15 min. before rinsing with cold water. It may help to work the paste in with an old toothbrush. Caution: Never use salt water to remove blood stains from carpets; you may rot the backing.

- Candle Wax . . . Lift blobs of candle wax from your fine wood furniture. A plastic credit card makes a good scraper, and one that won't scratch . . . OR . . . train your hair dryer (hottest setting) on the mess, working the wax off with a rubber spatula after softening.

- Candle Wax . . . To remove a candle wax stain, dab away as much of the softened wax as you can, using a paper towel or the credit card or spatula recommended in previous hint. Then cover the stain with several squares of clean white tissue, heating with a warm – not hot – iron. Replace with fresh tissues until no more wax can be absorbed.

- Chewing gum will lift off washable fabrics if you harden it first with an ice cube placed in a small plastic bag. Pick off as much as possible and then use grease spot remover to remove the last bits.

- Chocolate ... Sponge with cold water. Then rub gently with a solution of 1 tbsp. borax to 1 cup warm water. Rinse well and launder as usual.

- Coffee ... Sponge fresh stains with borax/water solution given above, then launder; rub glycerine into a stain that has set, laundering as usual. You may need a pre-spotter if there was cream in the cup.

- Coffee ... Lift fresh coffee, wine and fruit stains from most fabrics by stretching the stained area over a bowl and pouring boiling water over the stain from a height of two or three feet. Coffee stains with cream should be treated with a pre-spotter.

- Collar Stains ... Banish ring around the collar by brushing liquid shampoo onto the spot. An old toothbrush is ideal for the job. Then wash as normal.

- Fingerprints ... Gently erase fingerprints from good quality white paper by kneading a slice of soft white bread in your hand until it becomes doughy. Use the bread as a soft eraser.

- Fruit Stains ... To remove fruit, wine or blood stains from polished wood, sand finely and apply hydrogen peroxide sparingly to the marks. Clean and wax.

- Grass ... Soak overnight in cold water to which a little vinegar has been added ... OR ... work a little washing-up liquid directly onto the stain before laundering.

- Grease, car ... Work a little lard – yes, lard – onto the stain, allowing it to stand 30 min. before laundering. This method takes courage, but those who have tried it swear it works.

- Grease on suede leather ... Dust with finely ground oatmeal, rubbing gently with a clean, dry cloth. Repeat as needed, brushing when finished.

- Grease ... Remove soaked-in grease from finished wood furniture. Dust a generous layer of cornflour or talcum powder over the spot, applying clean white tissue paper over the powder. Apply an iron (low setting) over this, shifting the paper as you work, to absorb the grease. Don't let the iron touch the surface of the wood.

- Grime on suede leather ... Knead a slice of fresh, white bread until it's soft and pliable, rubbing it over the suede like a gentle eraser ... OR ... rub the spots gently with an emery board, holding them over a steaming kettle to refresh the nap.

- Hem Marks ... Remove the mark of an old hem by sponging with a warm vinegar and water solution, rinsing with clear water before pressing.

- Indian ink ... Lightly rub with petrol before laundering. And good luck! This one's a toughie.

- Ink stains ... Remove ink stains from most fabrics with office glue thinner.

- Ink stains will lift off fabrics soaked in milk as soon as possible after the accident occurs.

- Ink Stains ... Lift ink stains from a fine oak desk with ordinary household bleach. The method: remove the wood's finish and sand well, applying chlorine bleach to the stain and allowing to dry. Repeat until the stain lightens or disappears.

    Still more effective is oxalic acid, found in crystal form at some larger chemists. Add the crystals to hot water until no more can be dissolved, brushing the solution over the stain and allowing to dry until the crystals can be swept away. You may have to treat the entire surface of the wood to get an even colour; stain and refinish for perfect results.

7

- Iodine ... Rub with a cut lemon before washing in warm water.

- Lipstick ... Remove lipstick stains from most washable fabrics with pre-spotter or cleaning fluid, then bleach with a commercial product suitable for the fabric.

- Make up ... If you can't wash the stain right away, try an "eraser" made from a well-kneaded slice of very fresh white bread.

- Mildew ... You can sometimes remove mildew from a book by dusting lightly with cornflour and allowing it to remain on the pages several days.

- Mildew on coloured fabrics ... Soak and then wash in a strong detergent solution. Do not use chlorine bleach. Some staining may persist. With any mildew, try brushing off as much as possible, first.

- Mildew on leather ... Cover the area with Vaseline jelly, working it in well. Repeat. Let stand 24 hr. Shine with a clean, dry cloth.

- Mildew on tents and awnings ... Cover the area with Vaseline, working it in well. Repeat. Let stand 24 hr. Shine with a clean, dry cloth.

- Mildew on white cottons ... Soak in a strong chlorine bleach and water solution before laundering.

- Mustard ... Rub with a solution of warm water and baking soda. Then boil clean in a detergent solution to which 1 or 2 tsp. of ammonia have been added.

- Mustard and curry ... Will often lift off if they are rubbed

66

with a little glycerine before washing in a warm water solution.

- Oily stains on polyester garments ... A common laundry problem. Soak the garment overnight in a solution of ¼ cup powdered bleach to 2 qt. water. Then wash as usual. Never use chlorine bleach on polyesters.

- Paint, oil-based, dried ... Soak in a solution of ½ cup ammonia and ¼ cup turpentine for a least 20 min. Rinse and wash as usual.

- Perspiration stains should come out of washable fibres soaked for an hour in one quart of lukewarm water and ¼ cup salt.

- Perspiration and grease stains can usually be sponged off colourfast clothes before washing. Use full strength warm vinegar and they should vanish.

- Rust ... Clean rust from scissors by soaking several minutes in full-strength ammonia and wiping with a damp cloth.

- Rust ... To remove rust from clothing, rub a paste made from salt and lemon juice generously on the spot. Dry in the sun for two or three hours, rinsing well .. OR ... dab lemon juice and salt on the stains, stretching the fabric snugly over the steam from a boiling kettle. The rust will disappear in seconds: rinse well.

- Scorches, linens ... Will often disappear if you rub the mark with a freshly cut onion, releasing onion juices over it. Then soak in a mild solution of hydrogen peroxide and water (or plain water) several hours before laundering.

- Scorches, linens and white cottons ... Cover the area with a piece of cloth soaked in 3 per cent hydrogen peroxide, ironing directly over the moistened fabric.

- Scorches, wool ... If the mark is light, try rubbing it with an emery board or very fine sandpaper.

- "Shine" ... Remove "shine" from garments by sponging with a mixture of white vinegar and water and pressing on the wrong side.

- Spots ... Remove spots from most fabrics by rubbing with fizzy soda water.

- Tags ... Remove sticky price tags from surfaces that won't absorb oils by rubbing peanut butter into the remaining adhesive .. OR ... by pressing masking tape, sticky side down onto the "gunk" several times.

- Tea, fresh ... Sprinkle with salt before washing. If there was cream in the drink, you may need a pre-spotter.

- Water Rings ... remove white water rings from polished woods. Spirits of camphor on a moistened cloth will do it .. OR ... an application of plain white toothpaste, rubbed in with a dry cloth .. OR ... essence of peppermint .. OR ... a mixture of olive oil and cigar ash .. OR ... rubbing with the cut edge of a shelled Brazil nut. These treatments may also remove heat marks.

- Clean walls, car interiors, floors, bathrooms, windows, and rugs with this solution: Mix 1 gal. water, 1 cup white vinegar, ½ cup liquid ammonia, and ¼ cup washing soda. Store in old bleach bottles (out of kids' reach!) and keep a smaller washing-up liquid bottle of it handy.

- No need to buy costly drain cleaner. Make you own. Mix 1 cup bicarbonate of soda, 1 cup salt, and ¼ cup cream of tartar. Flush ¼ cup of this mixture down each drain once weekly, followed by 1 cup boiling water. Chase with a cold water rinse, and this should keep drains free of clogs and odours.

- The best home remedy for cleaning precious oil paintings is a freshly cut chunk of raw potato. Rub carefully across the canvas, trimming clean slices as it gets dirty. If you own the Mona Lisa, though, save the potatoes for vichyssoise. Have the thing professionally cleaned.

- This all-purpose spot remover is effective for many stains. Combine 2 parts water to 1 part rubbing alcohol. Test on a hidden patch of fabric before using.

Look Good...
Feel Good...
and Save Money

Clothes

- Here's how to raise the nap of velvet fabric. Steam it with a kettle, brushing lightly with another swatch of velvet – preferably the same colour as the fabric being brushed.

- Perk up your old fur coat. Shake on cornflour. Brush out with a baby's hairbrush.

- Iron your clothes as you shower – hang them in the bathroom.

- Iron your clothes as you sleep – pants and hankies can be pressed by laying them flat between your mattress and box spring.

- Protect your cupboards from moths. Dangle a sachet of well-dried orange peel from any convenient cupboard hook. The knotted leg of an old pair of tights makes a good container.

- Moths won't go near clothes stored in a box or chest lined with red cedar.

- Here's a fast wrinkle remover for all wool garments – just drape the outfit over a shower curtain rod while you luxuriate in the tub. The steam will freshen it immediately.

- Airline travellers – protect your tie while eating. Slip it into the plastic holder the cutlery comes in, or tuck it into your shirt.

- Dry a beret without shrinking it. Slip it over a dinner plate. The more snugly it fits, the better.

8

- Angora sweaters will shed less if they're stored in a plastic bag in the fridge.

- You'll get more wear from your tights if you spray the heel and toe with hairspray.

- Zippers won't stick if you run a soft graphite pencil up and down the teeth.

- Dust-proof seldom-worn suits and jackets by covering the shoulders with cut-down dry cleaner bags.

- Hang heavy garments by taping two or three regular hangers together. Saves buying a special heavy duty hanger.

Shoes

8

- Rain splatters will disappear from suede shoes that are gently rubbed with an emery board before a once-over with a stiff suede brush.

- Remove shiny spots from suede shoes by dabbing with vinegar, allowing to dry, and then going over each shoe with a stiff brush.

- Sponge salt stains from your boots and shoes by dabbing with a 50/50 solution of white vinegar and water. Remove all trace of vinegar with a clean, damp cloth.

- Soften cracked paste shoe polish by placing it and a cup of water in your microwave oven for about 45 sec. Make sure your brand of polish is the kind sold in a glass jar, however, and not in a metal container.

- Don't slip the light fantastic in new shoes. You'll step out with confidence if you lightly sandpaper the soles.

- Stretch a tight shoe. Thoroughly wet a couple of sheets of newspaper, balling into a "toe" shape and squeezing out as much moisture as you can. Stuff into the toe of your shoe and leave it there 48 hours – guaranteed to work OR ... jam a long potato into your shoe to help stretch it out.

- Line leaky boots with Styrofoam meat trays, cut to fit. The extra padding also keeps your feet a little warmer.

- Find your boots fast when you're one of a crowd. Boots and galoshes are easy to spot if you clip them together with a coloured plastic clothes peg, distinguishing them from all those other pairs on your host's mat.

- Clean brown leather shoes with the inside of a banana skin.

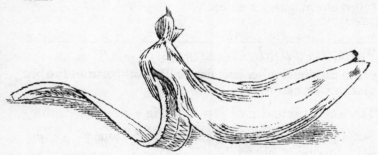

- Patent leather shoes and bags will sparkle after they've been wiped over with a vinegar-dampened cloth.

- Rub finger marks from patent leather by painting with fresh cold milk, allowing it to dry before buffing.

- Your shoes will have an extra gloss if you buff them with a thin sock after polishing. The warmth of your hand produces the extra sheen.

- Broken shoe lace tips will thread more easily if you dip them into clear nailpolish and allow them to dry first.

- Keep tennis shoes white by coating them with spray starch after washing.

71

- Polish sandals quickly by slipping a clean plastic bread bag over the hand that holds the shoe.

- Your shoes will really shine if they're buffed with a few drops of lemon juice.

- Dry wet boots with your hair dryer or the exhaust hose of your vacuum cleaner.

- Wet boots will stand straighter and dry more quickly if you insert a role of wire mesh in each.

- Make a simple shoe rack by mounting a curtain rod a few inches from the floor of your clothes cupboard .. OR ... using a cardboard box used for drink, with the dividers left in.

- Prevent fashionable knee-high boots from wrinkling by storing potato crisp cans, folded grocery bags, or rolled-up magazines in each.

Jewellery and Accessories

- Clean rings and other jewellery with toothpaste and an old mascara brush.

- To clean diamond jewellery, soak in gin.

- Buff up pearl necklaces by rubbing each stone with a very light coating of olive oil.

- Your claw-set jewellery will sparkle if it's soaked in a solution of warm water and bicarbonate of soda.

- Strengthen the thread of a newly-strung necklace with beeswax from your sewing box.

- The next time a favourite necklace breaks, re-string the beads on thread generously coated with hardened soap. The next time the thread breaks, a few beads may drop off, but most will be held fast by the soap.

- Before re-stringing the graduated beads of a broken necklace, lay them in the order in which they'll be strung, on a piece of Sellotape.

- Restore cloth flowers to their original cripsness by briefly holding them over the spout of a steaming kettle.

Face

- A good facial needn't be expensive – an egg white whipped frothy will work wonders. Leave on for 10 minutes, rinse with cool water and pat dry.

- For a great facial toner, mix a few drops of lemon juice with yoghurt ... but keep away from eyes.

- Or try an oatmeal facial combining one beaten egg yolk with 1 tbsp. cooked cooled oatmeal, 1 tbsp. honey, and ⅛ tsp. lemon juice. Pat on face, keeping away from eyes; rinse off after 20 min.

- Moisturize your skin by blending half a mashed banana with 1 tsp. honey. Leave on face 20 min.

- Tone up and moisturize tired skin with a carrot juice facial. Blend 2 tsp. carrot juice, an egg white (for oily skin) or an egg yolk (for dry skin), and 1 tbsp. honey. Leave on face 20 min. before rinsing.

- Need an astringent? Grapefruit juice is excellent .. OR ... pat buttermilk over your face, allow to dry, and rinse off with cool water.

- Blemishes will fade away if you dab a little lemon juice on them.

- Dead skin will peel off elbows, knees, feet, and face massaged with mayonnaise.

- Pack your bags – eye bags, that is – with dampened gauze squares filled with raw grated potato. This will temporarily eliminate puffiness around the eyes.

- Refresh tired eyes with slices of cucumber; keep them in place about 10 min. while you think pleasant thoughts.

Hair

- Condition your hair with a mashed, ripe avocado blended with just enough water to become creamy. Comb into scalp right to damaged ends. Leave on about 10 min. before rinsing with cool water.

■ Mayonnaise conditions the hair if rubbed in and left on under a plastic "tent" for 15 min. before shampooing. Rinse well and wash as usual.

■ Creme rinse your hair with a beaten egg yolk; rinse off with lukewarm – never hot! – water.

■ Remove all trace of soap and leave your hair silky by adding vinegar to your final hair rinse – just a little is all you need.

■ Lighten fair hair by adding a few drops of lemon juice to your final rinse after shampooing.

Hands and Feet and the Rest

■ Rid your nails of yellow nicotine stains by rubbing with a cottonwool ball dampened with lemon juice .. OR ... by brushing with a cotton-tipped swab coated with 20-volume peroxide and leaving on 10 min. (remove as soon as your nails start to feel tingly). Rinse with lukewarm water and apply hand cream to moisturize.

■ Clean nicotine stains from your fingernails by soaking a piece of fresh horseradish in cider vinegar for 48 hours, applying to nails and leaving on as long as you can. Rinse in lukewarm water.

■ Nails yellowed because you have neglected to apply a base coat under your polish must grow out before they will improve. Always protect them with a base coat once they whiten again.

■ Nail polish will spread more smoothly if it's stored in the fridge.

■ Gummy nail polish will soften up if you put the bottle in a pan of boiling water for a minute or two.

■ Soften your cuticles with a light coating of vegetable oil shortening. This also makes an excellent hand cream, and you don't need much of it.

■ Give your feet a treat. Three tablespoons of bicarbonate of soda mixed in a quart of warm water makes a fine foot bath – soak 10 or 15 min.

■ Bathing beauties will appreciate this yoghurt oil bath: Blend 1 cup oil with 1 cup yoghurt, storing in fridge. Add a few tablespoons to your bathwater and soak.

■ Make your own refreshing mouthwash with equal quantities of bicarbonate of soda and salt dissolved in a glass of warm water. One-half teaspoon of each is sufficient.

■ Whiten your elbows by resting each in a squeezed cut lemon half.

■ You'll cool down faster on hot days if you soak both wrists in cold water.

■ Store your cologne in the fridge when it's hot outside. It's very refreshing.

Making the Most of Cosmetics

■ Concoct your own mild shampoo by simmering leftover soap scraps in water until melted. If too thick, add more water. Cool and store at room temperature .. OR ... combine 1 cup Palmolive washing-up liquid, 1 cup vinegar (white vinegar for light hair, malt vinegar for dark), and ½ cup water. Store in plastic squeeze bottle.

■ Making your own soap isn't as hard as it sounds. Use 5 lb. (10 cups) lukewarm fat, saved and strained from roasts, chickens, and bacon, 1 lb. lye, 4 cups cold water, 1 tbsp. borax, 1 tsp. salt, 2 tbsp. sugar, ½ cup cold water, and ¼ cup ammonia. Melt fat and strain through cheesecloth. Dissolve the lye in cold water, adding fat slowly and stirring constantly. Add remaining ingredients (borax, salt, sugar, cold water, ammonia) to first mixture, stirring until thick and light coloured. Pour into cloth-lined pan. Mark into desired bar sizes before soap hardens. When hard, break apart and allow to dry well. These bars can be finely rasped and used as laundry soap.

75

- Save money on lipstick. At least one third of your lipstick is buried in the tube; buy a brush. It will more than pay for itself.

- End bits of lipstick can be mixed together in a small cosmetic jar and applied as lipstick or rouge.

- Get every drop of liquid moisturizers, cleaners, and hand lotion from the bottle by turning it upside down for a day. What's left will collect in the cap.

- Cleansing creams are expensive – baby lotion does the same job for less than half the price.

- Extend your dusting powder by mixing it with an equal amount of cornflour.

- Stretch your perfume by adding a little alcohol to the bottle.

- Save those empty eyeshadow jars for small quantities of cold cream, rouge, and other make-up necessities when you travel. A great space saver.

8

Kill
or
Cure

Remedies for Common Ailments

These home remedies are no substitute for sound medical advice and treatment. If problems persist, see your doctor, and don't waste a moment if you suspect something serious.

- Relieve your asthma by chewing the leaves of the comfrey plant. The leaves and roots can be used as a tea or poultice.

- Save your voice from the strain of laryngitis. Mix a thin mash of bran flakes or bran cereal with boiling water and enough honey to sweeten, downing this throughout the day to soothe your vocal chords.

- Bad beath? Chew a little parsley ... or a lot.

- Hiccup cures are numerous, but if you really want to stop those spasms, swallow a tablespoon of dry sugar or drink a glass of cold water while a friend plugs your ears.

- Or drink a shot of vinegar, in one swallow.

- A dollop of peanut butter helps stick the hic, too.

- Your gums won't bleed after minor dental surgery if you bite down hard on a damp gauze tea bag for one hour.

- Relieve sore breasts by abstaining from all caffeine-laced beverages and pain killers. This works in 8 women out of every 10, but allow 6 months for every trace of caffeine to disappear from your system. That means no tea, coffee, chocolate, or cola.

- Quit smoking by snacking on sunflower seeds. New medical studies reveal sunflower snackers find it easier to break the habit than those who try other methods.

9

77

- Nosebleed? Sit – don't lie down – pressing an ice cube in a plastic sandwich bag against the bleeding side of your nose. Pinch the other side closed as you're doing this.

- Can't get to sleep? Brew some tea from valerian roots. Or down a glass of warm milk.

- Double chin? Tighten it up by chewing gum 15 to 20 min. each day.

- Calm a jittery, woozy stomach by downing this brew. Just combine 1 tsp. bicarbonate of soda and a squeeze of lemon juice in a medium-sized glass of warm water.

- Try this headache remedy if you don't want to take a pill or tablet. Pop two whole cloves into a hot cup of tea, and sip.

- Try this old wives' treatment for boils. Rub a bar of household soap over the infected area; boils should disappear within a couple of weeks.

- Shrink mild hemorrhoidal swelling. One home remedy suggests you insert a peeled garlic clove gently into the rectum, about two inches up.

- Constipation will pass if you drink 6 to 8 glasses of water each day, and add 2 tbsp. natural bran to your diet. Prunes and prune juice are natural laxatives, too.

- Banish bunion pain with this old trick. Paint your bunions with a light coating of iodine each night for a week: Repeat if necessary.

- Ease an annoying fish bone down your throat, assuming it's a small one. Suck on a wedge of lemon, and it should dissolve more quickly.

- Here's a good old-fashioned syrup to soothe your irritated throat. Boil the juice of one lemon 10 min., adding it to 1 cup honey and 1 oz. glycerine. Stir well and take 1 tsp. three times daily. You may want to cut down on the glycerine slightly; it's a laxative.

- Mustard plasters won't blister tender skin if you use the unbeaten white of an egg instead of the water called for in the mixture.

- Here's how to make one: spread equal quantities of flour, mustard powder, and enough water to make a thick paste, on a double layer of cheesecloth. Position the plaster over skin that has first been protected with a generous lather of Vaseline. Cover the plaster with a clean, dry towel. Remove when the skin turns pink; do not use on sensitive skin, or on childrens' skin. Repeat as needed to loosen chest colds and ease muscle aches.

- Attention, mothers-to-be! Ease morning sickness by sucking a lemon wedge. It works!

- Lighten stretch marks during and after pregnancy. Rub coconut oil over them.

Warts

- Worried about your warts? Home remedies are numerous. You can try one of these cures, but remember this. About half of most common warts disappear on their own, within a year of their debut. You may not have to do anything at all.

  — Rub the wart with bacon rind, burying the rind in the ground. The wart should shrink to nothing while the rind rots in the soil.

  — Spit on the wart and rub it with a bar of laundry soap or with the head of a red-tipped match.

— Rub the wart with the cut side of a raw potato ... but only when the moon is full, at midnight.

— Work a little castor oil into it each morning and night, until it disappears.

— Mix a little powdered chalk with water, applying it to the wart. After this you wait. And wait some more.

— Plantar warts will sometimes vanish if you hold a hot cigarette ash near them – but never close enough to burn.

Stings and Sunburn

■ Take the sting from that nettle rash. Nettles usually grow near dock. Moisten the sting with spit and slap a dock leaf on it ... works like magic.

■ Soothe painful sunburn by patting it gently with mint-flavoured Milk of Magnesia.

■ Dab full-strength vinegar on mosquito bites – this stops the itch.

■ Relieve the sting of minor burns by dabbing with the white of an egg.

■ Relieve the pain of severe sunburn by pouring evaporated milk over the sore areas – but plug your nose! This smells dreadful ... but works .. OR ... dab with cottonwool soaked in vinegar .. OR ... apply a paste of bicarbonate of soda and water .. OR ... rub gently with cider vinegar .. OR ... apply yoghurt to your body and leave for 45 min.

80

Hangovers

■ A wise philosopher (and if I didn't have this headache, I'd remember who it was) once said that there's no cure for a hangover save death. He was probably right, though you can try:

— Covering your feet with cucumber slices, right up to the ankle.

— Slapping an ice pack of frozen peas over your throbbing head.

9

— Before going to bed, down one slightly beaten egg yolk in a glass of beer. On waking, drink a mixture of brandy, tomato paste, oil, vinegar, salt, and paprika in whatever proportions you can tolerate, chasing this with another egg yolk and a sprinkling of horseradish. One stipulation: The whole yucky concoction must be drunk in one gulp. Cheers!

— Or on waking force down 1 cup hot water, 2 dessert-spoonfuls cider vinegar, and 1 spoonful honey.

— You can also add 2 drops of Angostura bitters to a glass of soda water or Perrier, taking this before or after bed. Maybe next time you'll think twice about getting sloshed.

Splinters

■ Splinters work loose more easily if the area is soaked in warm olive oil before you try to remove them.

- A deeply imbedded splinter will also rise to the surface of your skin if you hold the affected area over the open mouth of a small jar or bottle filled with boiling water. The steam will draw the sliver to the surface, where it can be tweezed free.

- You'll always have an emergency needle handy for coaxing out slivers if you tape a Bandaid inside the door of your medicine chest, poking the needle into the padded part.

Help for Harassed Mums

- Soothe baby's upset tummy with camomile tea, made from the flowers of the plant.

- Relieve baby's nappy rash, prickly heat, and other mild skin irritations by adding 2 tbsp. bicarbonate of soda to his bath water.

- Use socks for pox. Sleeping children won't scratch chicken pox and measles if you slip a pair of socks over their hands.

- Children swallow pills more readily if they're rolled in peanut butter, first. The pills, that is – not the children.

- A handy way to rest a spoon over a child's medicine glass and avoid marking the night table is to wrap a rubber band lengthwise up and over the top of the glass. The band holds the spoon snug – no danger of flipping off.

And other Useful Things to Know

- Bitter medicine goes down more smoothly if the intended sucks an ice cube, first. This deadens the taste buds.

- Pluck out that cottonwool nestled deep in your medicine bottle. Use a crochet hook.

- The label of your medicine bottle will always be easy to read if you protect it with a coat of clear nail polish. Spills wipe right off.

- Sickbed patients will know the time but won't be bothered by the ticking if you invert a drinking glass over a watch on the dressing table, or cover a clock with a clear glass mixing bowl.

- Shaving nicks won't stain your collar if you stem the flow of blood by dipping a moistened finger into a little pow-dered alum, dabbing this on the cut.

And Baby Makes Three

The First Year

- The best unscented baby powder for youngsters with sensitive skin is plain cornflour.

- Shampoo won't drip into baby's eyes if you rub a little Vaseline around his brows.

- Grip small babies firmly in the bathtub by donning an old cotton glove on the hand holding baby.

- Drinking cups won't slip from baby's hand if you wrap an elastic band over the base and another slightly further up.

- Cut-up disposable nappies make excellent nursing pads for mum.

- Unsoiled nappy liners can be washed and re-used several times for baby's bottom.

- Baby's car potty will be much simpler to clean if you line it with a plastic bag.

- Baby's rubber pants will stay soft and pliable after washing if you add a drop of liquid paraffin to the rinse water and never, never toss in the dryer.

- Baby's first bed will look even prettier if you trim it with your wedding lace. Presto! An heirloom.

- Babies feel safer in the tub when they're bathed in a plastic laundry basket. The loose plastic mesh lets the water swish freely through, while giving baby something to cling to.

10

- Warm baby's midnight bottle without turning on the stove. Pour some of the water from the evening's earlier bottle warm-up into a preheated vacuum bottle. When it's late and you're tired, empty the water from the flask into a pan holding the bottle, allowing the milk to warm while you change the baby's nappy.

The Second Year

- Toddler-proof your kitchen cupboard doors. Latch two shower curtain hooks together, looping them through the handles.

- Toddlers feel more confident in new shoes if the soles have been roughed up with fine sandpaper.

And After

- Double the life of your youngster's crayons. Wrap a strip of masking tape around each while they're still new.

10

- Entertain youngsters inexpensively on a rainy afternoon. Make a habit of saving the weekend comics – the kids won't remember what they read months ago, and will enjoy the treat.

- Children won't slip off swing seats decorated with rubber bathtub motifs.

- Don't dump that garden swing kids have outgrown. With the seat and supports gone, it makes an excellent A-frame base for a playhouse.

- Right up your alley for a rainy day. Set up empty bottles, trying to knock them over with a soft ball. The kids will love their own bowling lane in the hallway of your house.

- Children's iron-on patches will stay in place longer if you slip a sheet of foil inside the pant leg as you press it on. The foil reflects extra heat back to the patch, strengthening the bond.

- Calm a tantrum by whispering to your child – he'll stop the ruckus to hear what you're saying.

- Children who hate carrots will gobble them up when they're mashed – or sneaked into carrot cakes.

- Outsmart your quarrelling kids. They will soon be giggling if you assign them a window to wash – one on the inside, the other on the outside.

- Children will keep their clothes neater if you screw a towel rack to the foot of each bed.

- Keep little ones busy with a sandpaper "drawing board" and some coloured wool. The wool will cling to the board and can quickly be "erased" and formed into new pictures.

- Old socks make excellent hand puppets for children.

- Store building blocks and other small toys in economy size coffee tins covered with adhesive-backed paper.

- Jigsaw puzzle pieces won't go astray if you colour-code each piece of each complete puzzle with a crayon, allowing you to separate jumbled puzzles in a flash. Store individual puzzles in plastic bags.

- Read your child a bedtime story even when you're busy doing something else. The next time you sit down to read aloud, keep a small cassette recorder close by. Then when you don't have time to read on some future occasion your child can still doze off to a bedtime tale as you play back the cassette.

- You can find the matching mate to your child's boots if you put a small strip of coloured tape on the back of each. It's easy to match up the colours, even in a pile of look-alikes in the school cloak-room.

- Kids won't go wild with the shampoo if you transfer it from its original bottle to a clean, empty hand-lotion bottle with a pump nozzle. One "pump" is enough.

- Coax chewing gum from hair with a little peanut butter or cold cream .. OR ... freeze it with an ice cube.

- Sick children confined to bed enjoy small meals served in a bun tin. Each of the cups can hold something to nibble on, and a small drinking cup fits snugly, too.

- Children confined to bed won't spill drinks served in a screw-top jar with a hole in the lid just large enough for a drinking straw.

10

- When your sick child gets restless in bed, allow him to have a "picnic" by snipping colourful magazine pictures of foods he'd like to eat (but can't). The game will keep him occupied as he assembles the "meal", and you can "dine" with him when he's through clipping.

Sew and Knit

Children's Clothes

- Your little girl's bathing suit will be good for one more season if you cut it in two pieces across the middle, sewing a neat hem and elastic in each half. Voila! A two-piece bathing suit.

- Children will outgrow their coats and jackets less quickly if you sew knitted cuffs (available in haberdashery departments) into the sleeves.

- Children's new trousers will wear longer if you apply iron-on patches to the inside of the knees before they're worn.

11

- Brownie, Guide, Scout and school badges will stay straight while you sew them on if you dab washable glue on the wrong wide and allow it to set before you begin stitching.

- Make cheap blackout curtains for baby's room by securely pinning dark plastic dustbin liners to the inside of your curtains. Keep out of reach, though!

Make Do and Mend

- Recycle old bedsheets by cutting them into pillowcases.

- Don't trim a too-long slip at the bottom. Cut it at the waist, converting it to a half slip and camisole.

- Save fabric scraps, joining them in squares and stitching into a quilt that's uniquely yours.

- Trim old tablecloths into a number of napkins.

Tidy Ideas

- Round up stray pins in your sewing box by keeping a small magnet within easy reach.

- Your spools will stay neat in your sewing-box if you store them in wide-topped plastic pill bottles.

- Your sewing area will be neater if you tape a paper bag to the side of your sewing box or machine while you're working. Stray threads and snippets of fabric can be brushed directly into it, rather than littering the floor.

- The floor foot pedal of your sewing machine may travel farther than you do in a year. Stop it from creeping by gluing a thin piece of foam rubber to its underside.

- To keep scatter rugs from slipping and carpet edges from curling, see Carpet Care on page 22.

11

Useful Tips

- Mend a torn glove finger using a marble as a darning base.

- Keep buttons secure by dabbing with a drop or two of colourless nail polish after stitching – but don't try this on rayon-acetate fabrics.

- Sewing needles will slip through fabrics if you use a cake of soap as your pin cushion.

- Sew on a snap fastner ... in a snap! Just stitch the bumpy part on first: mark the bump with white chalk, and press it where it will fasten when closed. The chalk mark will tell you precisely where to centre the other half.

- Your knitting won't unravel if you snap a clothes peg over your needles each time you tuck them away. No dropped stitches.

- Keep your wool clean as you knit. Place it in a small bag tied loosely with a small scrap of wool or elastic band. The wool will unravel as you work, and will stay in one place, too.

Pet's Corner

Cats

- Give your cat a treat and cut a few calories from your diet at the same time by feeding it the skin of your chicken – as long as it isn't highly seasoned. That's the fatty part, and avoiding it will do wonders for your waistline while making your cat's coat gleam. Make sure he never gets a chicken bone, though.

- Deodorize your cat's litter box by sprinkling 1 part bicarbonate of soda on the bottom and topping with 3 parts litter. This is nothing to sniff at! It's effective.

- Discourage the cat from cuddling up on the sofa by tucking a few mothballs in between the cushions.

- Liven up dry cat food by pouring tinned fish oil onto it.

- Want to break your cat of the costly habit of eating only those small tins of "gourmet" cat food? A cold turkey switch to a cheaper product probably won't work – your pet will go on a hunger strike before touching it or any other food he hasn't become accustomed to. Change his habits by mixing a gradually larger proportion of the other food with the gourmet brand each day, so that he is unaware of the switch.

- Discourage cats from scratching the furniture. Put two-sided sticky tape over their favourite spots, and they'll give up when they find their paws start to stick.

- "Nail" your cat when he scratches the furniture. What he's really doing is marking his territory with a faint scent exuded from the pads of his feet. Move the furniture and put his scratching post in the same spot for a while.

12

91

- Don't let your summer travels become your cat's travails. Your cat will be more comfortable in the car if you drape cold towels over his carrier.

- Your cat will enjoy snoozing in a seldom-used laundry basket padded with a cushion. Just cut it down on one side.

- Cats won't return to a favourite wetting spot if the area is lightly sprayed with cologne.

- Cat catastrophes can be treated in the same manner as doggie accidents on the rug, but once the spot is dry, rub gently with an ammonia-dampened cloth. The cat will not return to the same spot.

Dogs

- Rid your pet of fleas by sprinkling ½ tsp. of brewer's yeast over his food every day. Washing your dog in salt water will also help keep fleas at bay, as will garlic powder, lightly sprinkled on his dinner.

- Your dog will enjoy a foam rubber mat in his house. Fleas won't nest in the foam as they will in cloth.

- Kill your dog's ticks with a blob of Vaseline. They'll fall off his hide as their air supply it cut off.

- Deodorize the dog between baths by brushing bicarbonate of soda through his fur.

- Giving your pet a pill is easier if you hide it in a chunk of soft food.

- Quieten a crying puppy by tucking an old alarm clock, wrapped in a towel, into his basket with him. Almost as good as mum.

- Dogs avoid rubbish bags sprayed with ammonia.

- Doggie accidents on the rug should be blotted up and rubbed with a solution of vinegar and warm water. Follow this with a liberal dose of soda water, rubbing gently. Blot thoroughly.

12

- Dogs adore these homemade biscuits: Mix two jars of strained beef baby food with ¼ cup skimmed milk powder and ½ cup wheat germ. Flatten small balls on lightly-greased cookie sheet and bake at 350 degrees F. until light brown.

- Reduce your dog's shedding and condition his coat to a new lustrous sheen. Feed him a daily dose of 1 to 3 tsp. corn oil, mixed into his regular diet.

- Your dog's coat will be soft and silky if you add two raw eggs to his food each week.

- If your pet's white coat is stained, wipe a 3 per cent hydrogen peroxide solution on the darker areas, squeezing out the excess and immediately dusting with a light brushing of cornflour. Brush again when dry, repeating every other day until the stain lightens or disappears altogether, and later cleaning with warm water only. If the stain reappears, treat with peroxide once more, keeping the solution well away from eyes.

- Stains on your pet's whiskers and beard will lift off if you fill a plastic squeeze bottle with equal parts of Fuller's Earth and cornflour, squirting some of this onto the area before brushing it out. This kills odours, too.

12

Cage Birds

- Budgies won't talk with a second bird or mirror in their cage, which may be the reason why your bird is mum.

- Encourage your budgie to bathe. Tie a sprig of well-watered parsley to the bars of his cage and he'll peck at it, roll it around, and clean himself as well as if he'd dived into a tub.

- Tea time for birdie. A drink of cold, strong tea will check your bird's non-infectious diarrhoea. Replace the water in his dish with the brew.

Garden Birds

- Help the wild birds feather their nests. Tuck some fluff from your tumbler dryer or some of your dog's hair into their feeder.

- Attract birds to your birdbath by lining the bowl with brightly coloured marbles.

12

- Try this economical winter bird feeder. Save enough rendered fat to fill a small cardboard milk carton, adding a generous scoop of wild bird seed to it as the fat melts on the stove. When the mixture is good and thick, fill the milk carton and chill until solid. With the fat hardened, peel away the carton and dangle your feathered friends' dinner from a mesh bag such as those in which onions and garlic cloves are sold.

- Swallows won't nest in your eaves and sample your fruit trees if you hang strips of foil in their favourite spots.

- Make a simple birdfeeder by wrapping two wire clothes hangers around an old rectangular cake tin. Tape the tin to the inside of the hangers and string on your clothes line, away from prowling cats.

And Other Household Pets

- Neighbours pets and even visiting pigeons will steer clear of your garden and window sills if you dissolve 2 tbsp. moth flakes in ¾ cup paint thinner, spraying the solution on sills and other sites.

- Silverfish will make a fast exit from your house if you sprinkle epsom salts (magnesium sulphate) along the base of your walls and in crevices and corners.

- Repel moths from your cupboards by placing a few moth-balls in an old pair of tights and draping on a hanger. You can also dangle a few mothballs in a tea infuser.

- Spray a fly or wasp with hair lacquer; it works every bit as well as insecticide.

- A bee sting will hurt less if you tape a freshly sliced onion to the spot. And a bicarbonate of soda and water paste will take down the swelling.

- The most effective insect repellents contain a high percentage of diethyl toluamide. The more of this ingredient, the longer the repellent will last and the more protection it will give.

12

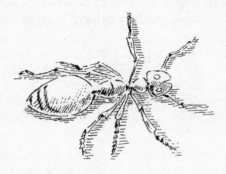

- Keep ants away from your picnic site with a simple chalk line – those outside the line won't cross it. Those already inside the line ... well, pack a little extra food for the picnic.

- Ants will make a beeline from your house if you put a few cucumber peelings in those spots they like to frequent.

- Here's a sure way to get rid of ants from your property: Mix ½ cup syrup, ¼ cup sugar, and ¼ cup dry yeast, stirring to a paste. Coat pieces of cardboard with this solution and place in ant runways.

- Finish off those lice without boiling bed sheets and clothes. Stuff everything that needs disinfecting (except people and pets, of course) into your microwave oven for 1 min. Be sure to add a cup of water, too, so the rays won't bounce back against the magnetron tube.

- Using your finger, draw a ring of concentrated flea shampoo solution around your pet's neck before plunging him into his bath and scrubbing him down. The shampoo rings kills those crafty fleas that make a dash for the safety of your pet's ears, where water and shampoo won't reach them.

- Fleas won't nest in rugs under which a few moth crystals have been sprinkled.

- Four-legged prowlers won't raid dustbins sprayed with ammonia or sprinkled with a little cayenne pepper.

- Mice and squirrels will steer clear of attics and spaces in which a few aromatic mothballs have been placed.

12

Car
Sense

Emergencies

- Fan belt snap: A pair of tights makes a good substitute; cut it to fit.

- A hot radiator cap is easier to twist off if you tuck an old pot holder into your car's tool box.

- If your radiator boils over and you need a container for water, use a hubcap.

- Strap a sagging exhaust in place with a bent coat hanger.

- Find that leak in your tyre by spraying with soapy water or shaving cream and watching for bubbles.

- If rusted wheel lug nuts make tyre changing more of a chore than it already is, slip a length of pipe over your wrench for extra leverage.

- If your car's stuck in snow with no help in sight, your floormats ... OR ... an old carpet stored in the boot ... will provide the added traction you need under your rear wheels.

- You'll always have a magnet if you keep a screwdriver in your glove compartment and magnetize it first.

- And here's what to do when the jump leads don't quite reach. Assuming both cars have negative ground (and 99 per cent of all cars do) and steel bumpers, make sure the bumpers are touching, to give a common ground. Then clip one jump lead to the other, attaching this single long cable to the positive terminals of both batteries. The conked-out car should start.

13

■ If you can't trust your battery, back into your garage. If your battery quits, you'll be closer to the jump leads if they're needed. Rear-motor car drivers please disregard.

Cleaning

■ To clean car chrome, rub with dampened aluminium foil. The chrome will be nice and shiny while the foil will turn black.

■ Wash your car with washing-up liquid. It won't scratch the surface.

■ Make clean-ups easier when it's time to do a greasy job under the hood. Rub cold cream into your hands before you get them grimy, and the dirt will wash right off.

■ Clean your car's windscreen with the ashes from your ashtray. Streaks and smudges disappear ... it's a pity the same doesn't apply to your lungs.

■ Tar and bugs will gently drip from a car sprayed with laundry pre-wash solution.

■ Keep the rim of your spare tyre from rusting and keep the tyre clean, too. Wrap the whole tyre in a large plastic bag before returning it to its storage spot.

■ Clean your car's sporty convertible top – rub the marks gently with a rubber. Sprayed-on fabric protector keeps that top looking newer, longer.

■ Restore tired vinyl car roofs to their original lustrous beauty. Work in a generous coating of Vaseline, repeating a week or two later. Miraculous!

13

- Keep the chamois you use to buff your car soft and supple by adding a few drops of olive oil to the rinse water after washing it.

- Bumper stickers will lift off if you work nail polish remover or hot vinegar around the edges – keep away from paint.

Coping in the Freeze-up

- Free a frozen car lock by plugging a hair dryer into the nearest outlet, training the hot blast on the lock. This, of course, works best in your own garage. You can't borrow a dryer when your car is frozen solid when you're miles from home.

- 'Snow fun when you're stuck in foul weather. A bag of cat litter stored in your boot will not only provide extra weight when you need it, but will give you extra traction when it's sprinkled under the wheels.

- Never set your hand-brake when your car is parked in a flat driveway or garage in winter. If the temperature drops too far, your brake drums could freeze, resulting in costly repairs.

- Putting chains on your wheels in the snow is less troublesome if first you jack up the car, resting the jack on the wheel rim of your spare tyre. This will raise the wheel above most snowdrifts.

- Scare sleeping cats from your car by giving your bonnet a hearty thump before you put the key in the ignition. Cats like to curl up against the engine block on cold mornings.

13

Other Useful Tips

- Remove a large concave dent from the door of your car without going near a garage. A bathroom plunger will often pop it out.

- Save an expensive repair job when your carburetor jets are plugged. Blow them out with a tyre pump.

- Car battery terminals will not corrode if they're greased with Vaseline.

- To remove any corrosion already present, pour on a bicarbonate of soda and water solution, or any fizzy pop, or soda water.

- A twice-yearly tuneup will pay for itself in saved petrol costs and improved engine performance.

- Save petrol by turning your car's engine off if you expect to idle 30 seconds or more. Provided you don't rev. the engine when you start up again, turning on the ignition does not – as some people think – use extra fuel.

- Squeaky fan belt? Squirt the inside of the belt with hair spray, increasing its friction and stopping the squeak.

- Rid your driveway of oil spots by sprinkling with cat litter and then sweeping .. OR ... by spreading several thicknesses of wet newspaper on the spots and allowing them to absorb the oil. Remove the papers when they are dry.

13

And Don't Forget

- You'll always know when your car needs servicing if you use this handy reminder. Clip a sturdy index card to your sun visor, noting the date, mileage, and work done each time.

- Always keep last year's phone book in your car. You'd be surprised how often it will come in handy.

- Say goodbye to parking panic when you always have a store of silver coins in a covered box under the dashboard for just such emergencies.

- Cigarettes won't go astray in the car if you slip a small magnet into the pack. It will adhere to any metal surface close at hand.

- Glue a small plastic pen holder to the glove compartment of your car and you'll never have to dig for a pen.

13

Gardening Time

Seeds

- Start seeds in discarded paper drinking cups with the bottoms removed, transplanting directly to pots or the garden as they grow.

- Plant small seeds with an eye dropper or mix with sand in a salt shaker and sprinkle out – the sand will help thin them.

- Transplant seedlings with an old ice cream scoop rather than a trowel. Each plant hole will be the same depth.

- Start seedlings in the half shell. An eggshell filled with potting soil makes an excellent first home for a seedling which can later be transplanted outside, still in its shell. As the shell disintegrates, it feeds the plant.

- Protect rows of tender seedlings from frost by laying half-rounds of gutter pipe over them.

- Cats won't scratch your seedlings if you drop sweetpea netting over them. The young plants will easily grow through the holes in the net, and animals will stay clear because they don't like getting their paws caught.

- Lettuce will grow up to four time faster under red glass than it will in direct sunlight. Beans flourish under red glass, too.

- Don't toss out those old seeds. They may still germinate. To find out for sure, place any 10 on a damp piece of cotton or on a damp blotter in a covered dish. You'll know what percentage will germinate in less than a week.

- Mix a little flour with your grass seed. You'll see where you've sown at a glance.

14

- Seeds grow best when planted in a waxing – never waning – moon. Lunar rhythms, say scientists, definitely affect plant growth.

- Sprout some parsley on your kitchen sill, by sprinkling a few seeds over a damp sponge.

Young Plants

- Guard tender young bedding plants from evening frost and heavy rains. A very simple method is to place sturdy stakes about 18 in. apart, on opposite sides of the planting row. Curve a sheet of corrugated flexible plastic between the stakes, and it will form a natural arch that is anchored in place on two sides.

- Stake tender saplings without hurting them. Thread a sturdy wire or straightened coat hanger through a length of old garden hose and you'll have twist-on supports that expand as the tree grows.

- Stake your plants before they need it and you won't damage the mature roots later.

- Plant anything that grows below the ground when the moon is waning. Plant anything that grows above the ground in a waxing moon.

Shrubs

- Outdoor shrubs will develop healthy leaves if they're sprinkled with a handful of epsom salts in the early spring.

- Camellias bloom best with epsom salts sprinkled underneath them.

- Hydrangeas will bloom pink if you work some nitrate of potash into the ground. They'll stay white if you add 1 tbsp. epsom salts to their drinking water. And they'll flourish with attractive blue blossoms if they're given a little sulphate of iron or aluminium. Whatever your colour choice, doctor these plants in mid-spring.

14

103

Potting Compost and Fertilizers

■ Get potted for next to nothing! Mix equal quantities of compost and vermiculite for a perfect growing medium. Start by sterilizing your well-rotted and sifted compost for 30 min. in a 200 deg. F. oven. You can also make a potting soil mix from equal quantities of peat moss and sand or equal parts of peat moss, vermiculite, and perlite.

■ Testing topsoil quality is best done in a science lab, but here's a quick way to get some idea of what you're buying. Fill a glass jar halfway with soil, top with clear water, cap, and shake vigorously. The soil and other materials in the jar will settle in layers, according to their specific gravity, so you can gauge the percentage of each material present in the sample. Small stones will settle to the bottom first, followed by a layer of sand, a layer of silt and clay particles, vegetable matter such as peat, a layer of water, and floating matter such as unrotted wood.

■ Make a mini compost heap in your kitchen. Grind celery stalks, asparagus and broccoli tips, and other vegetable matter directly into a covered bucket, sprinkling a little topsoil over this. Before you know it, the vegetables will have broken down to a very rich soil.

■ Fertilize your roses with wood ash from your fireplace.

■ Fertilize other plants and drive insects away by digging cold, used tea leaves into the soil at the base of the plant.

■ Ferns, lilies, and bromeliads will grow faster and stronger if you put them on The Pill. Dissolve one birth control pill in one quart of water and wet them with this solution – it really works!

14

Weeding

■ Kneel in comfort as you tend your plants. Cut strips of an old garden hose, strung together to form a good kneeling pad.

- Or kneel on a plastic rubbish bag, stuffing weeds into it as you work and making your perch even softer.

- Cushion your tender knees as you work in the garden. Sew half-inch elastic to a pair of old pot holders and slip them under your work pants.

- Dig up small weeds with an apple corer. You'll catch the roots but won't disturb the surrounding foliage.

- Storing bulbs over winter is no problem if you hang them in an old pair of tights.

- Conquer couch grass for once and for all. Sow a thick carpet of turnip or tomato seeds over it, and it will disappear.

- There's nothing dandy about dandelions. One natural way to kill them is to snip them off, close to the root, just before they flower. Then – and never mind the neighbours, who will surely think you've gone mad – harvest as many dandelions as you can find from hedgerows, laying them over the fleshy part of the root exposed on the surface of the ground. The root should wither up and die.

- Kill stubborn grass poking through garden paths and driveway cracks by pouring boiling salted water over them, and salting to prevent new growth .. OR ... pour chlorine bleach directly on it.

Pest Control

- Repel slugs with seaweed straight from local shores. A damp seaweed border is effective around flower beds and vegetables; dug into the ground, it will enrich the soil.

- Slugs will avoid a garden ringed with a light sprinkle of moth crystals (not moth balls).

- Rid outdoor plants of pests by mixing a liberal dose of soap flakes (nor detergent), ¼ tsp. vinegar, and about 4 cups water, spraying on the affected areas.

- Clobber club root before it hits your cabbages, cauliflower, Brussel sprouts, and broccoli. Add 1 tsp. white

14

vinegar to each gallon of water as you plant these. And cabbages are also less likely to develop this affliction if you lay a few stalks of rhubarb in the planting beds.

■ Cabbage flies will avoid plants ringed with a creosote-soaked string, laid on the surface of the soil .. OR ... plants whose young roots are bound with strips of aluminium foil.

■ Tomato pests including worms and flies will avoid plants grown near fresh basil. Dill also repels the tomato worm; garlic discourages blight.

■ Bugs won't bother your beets and carrots if you sow onions close to them.

■ The larvae of the carrot fly won't attack plants that have creosote-soaked string running along each row. Avoid larvae in the soil by mixing ground mothballs or crystals into the earth around the plantings.

■ Worms won't attack your carrot, onion, and radish seedlings if you sprinkle the planting rows with epsom salts, ringing grown plants with it, too.

■ The asparagus beetle will head for a neighbour's garden if you plant tomatoes near your asparagus.

■ Tough luck for the cucumber beetle – he'll go hungry if you plant radishes near your cukes.

■ Slugs will avoid your garden if:

— You plant spinach in your beds.

— You work a little chimney soot into and through the soil.

— You protect your plantings with a border of sawdust, fireplace ashes, damp seaweed, or moth crystals.

— You pour them a drink of beer. They're secret tipplers and love a little nip. Just pour some in a saucer; they'll crawl right in and drown.

Pest Control

■ Get rid of scaly plant bugs with lethal certainty. Add a

little rubbing alcohol from the chemist to your insecticide. The alcohol carries the pesticide past the bugs' waxy protective shells and into their systems.

- Your vegetable plot will have fewer bugs if you grow nasturtiums, asters, chrysanthemums, and geraniums around it. Each repels insects.

- Or spray your outdoor plants with this natural bug repellent. Soak cigar and cigarette butts in cold water for several hours, filling a spray bottle with this solution. Bugs won't go near a plant treated this way.

- Kill creepy crawlers that eat your plants and nest in the soil by giving them a dose of powdered mustard. Outdoors, mix 1 tbsp. per gallon of water; indoors, douse houseplants with 1 tsp. per gallon of water.

- Bid adieu to nematodes, white fly, and bean beetles. Plant marigolds around your vegetable patch.

- Potato bugs won't snack on spuds planted near horseradish.

- Potato blight won't stand a chance if you plant garlic nearby.

- Keep beetles from raiding your raspberries – plant garlic nearby.

- Cabbage whites won't invade your cabbage, Brussels sprouts, or broccoli if you grow dill, thyme, mint, or sage nearby.

14

- Discourage moles from burrowing through your garden by using this sneaky tactic. Bury beer bottles (or any other kind of bottle with a narrow neck) in the garden just up to their tops, so the wind whistles over them to create a low whooshing sound. If you bury the bottles where the moles are tunnelling, the noise should scare them off.

- Protect your slug bait from the rain. Cut three V-shaped notches into the lip of an empty cottage cheese container, inverting this carton over your bait. Slugs will crawl in to dine on their last supper.

- Lure earwigs from your vegetable garden by leaving a rolled-up newspaper near your plants overnight. Earwigs will nest inside; toss the paper in the fire the next morning.

- Aphids will avoid roses planted beside a single garlic clove. If you don't allow the garlic to flower, there won't be any smell. Chives help, too.

- Worms will depart your potted plants if you know how to draw them out. Hide a single slice of raw potato just under the surface of the soil; it will attract any worms.

- You can also drive worms from your plants by burying several matches in the soil, sulphur tip down.

- Fruit fly moths won't buzz around trees draped with jars containing a small amount of syrup and a drop of water. The flies are attracted to the sweetness and will drown in the water.

- Attract earthworms to your shaded shrubs. Spread a few damp coffee grounds under the plants.

- Rabbits won't nibble on plants ringed with a dusting of talcum powder; they detest the smell. Rabbits don't like mothballs, either, so take your choice.

- Rabbits and deer won't chew the tender bark of trees guarded with a collar of wire mesh.

- Deer also avoid plants inside a fence to which clumps of creosote-soaked rags have been tied.

14

Cut and Dried Flowers

■ Cut flowers will last longer if you add a pinch of sugar to the bottom of the vase. A penny or an aspirin in the vase have the same effect.

■ Lengthen the flowers' life by putting them in the fridge each night.

■ Cut roses will bloom longer if you slice the stem on a sharp angle and peel away the last couple of inches. Then – and I'm not kidding! – stand the entire stem (but not the buds or flowers) upright in very hot, but not boiling, water. Let flowers remain there until water is cool, and transfer to a vase with cold water.

■ Revive drooping roses the same way.

■ Flowers should be cut with a sharp knife rather than scissors, which squeeze the stem.

■ Food colouring will tint flowers prettily if you let them soak in coloured water overnight.

■ Autumn leaves will remain glossy and won't dry out if you add 2 oz. of glycerine to the water in their vase.

■ Lengthen flower stems cut too short for an arrangement with plastic drinking straws.

■ Mend a cracked vase by pouring liquid paraffin wax over the crack and allowing it to harden.

■ To hold flowers upright in a tall vase, criss-cross sticky tape over the top and poke the stems in between .. OR ... tie a few hair rollers together, popping the stems into them at the bottom of the vase.

■ Cut flowers will remain fresher longer if you add a small spoonful of washing soda to the water.

■ Fresh flowers deserve fresh water. Change it with your kitchen baster.

■ Drying flowers isn't difficult and will bring added beauty to your home even in the winter months. Here's how: Mix one part borax with two parts dry limestone sand, combin-

14

ing well. Pour some of this mixture into an oblong box large enough to hold two freshly cut flowers – flowers that have been in water with a preservative will not dry using this method. Make sure the flowers you choose have as little surface moisture clinging to them as possible.

Pour some of the borax mixture into the box (a shoebox with a lid is ideal) and gently place the flowers on top. If, like roses, your flower has overlapping petals, gently pour some of the borax mixture inside the centre of the petals. Cover the flowers (no more than two per box) with borax mixture, leaving no air space around the petals, leaves, or stem. Seal the box with tape, storing in a dark, cool place for 7 to 10 days ... judge how long according to the weather.

At the end of this time, carefully pour off enough of the borax mixture until you can see the flower, gently lifting it from the box and brushing off the last remaining particles of powder with a soft artist's brush.

- Drying flowers in your microwave oven is easier than you think. Roses, carnations, daffodils, pansies, and wild flowers work best; chrysanthemums, dahlias, and any flowers with thick centres do not dry satisfactorily. The method: Half-fill a 13×9-inch glass casserole dish with silica gel, gently laying flowers in it. Sprinkle more silica gel on top, covering leaves, stems, and petals completely so that no area is exposed. Make sure the centre of the flower is filled with gel, too.

  Put the dish into your microwave oven with 1 cup water at the back of the appliance. Heat 30 to 60 sec. before testing, depending on the size and texture of the flower. Flowers should be partially dry, and will continue drying for 10 to 15 min. more after they leave the oven. When flowers are completely dry, carefully remove each from the gel, using a fine brush to flick the remaining specks of silica from each petal.

Houseplants

- Houseplants that pine for sun during the long winter months will perk up nicely if they're allowed to bask

14

under an ordinary fluorescent light for several hours each day.

- The leaves of your houseplants will be just a little greener if you give them a monthly drink of plain household ammonia, diluted 1 tsp. to 1 gallon of water.

- Here's a decorative stake for houseplants that grows as they do. Use an expandable brass curtain rod.

- Stake small houseplants with cheap wooden chopsticks.

- Train your bonsai branches with straightened paper clips rather than costly copper wire.

- Perk up your plants by watering them with stale soda water.

- Window boxes will weigh less if you put potted plants in them rather than adding plants to a box of soil. The appearance is identical.

- Window boxes won't splatter your windows if you put a shallow layer of gravel over the earth.

- A flower pot will hold its soil better and will drain more slowly if you plug its drain hole with a four-slot button, a bottle cap, or a piece of cut-up sponge.

- Flower pots won't topple off a narrow window ledge if they're held secure by a "guard rail" made from a curtain rod.

- Buff up waxy plant leaves with a few drops of liquid paraffin dissolved in water, applying with cotton wool or cotton buds .. OR ... try a light coating of castor oil.

- Hold water in your plant pots by placing a few cut-up sections of sponge at the bottom.

14

- Your plants will enjoy good drainage if you use a broken clay pot, some marbles, a few small rocks, or a little charcoal before adding earth.

- Cold leftover tea (hold the cream and sugar, please!) is a treat for houseplants, as is a tablespoon of castor oil (only occasionally) followed by a good watering.

- Hanging plants that drip when watered will make less mess if you snap a shower cap over the base of the pot, catching run-offs.

- Water houseplants from a container into which you've dropped a few broken eggshells.

- Going on holiday? You can still water your plants. Place them in the bath on wet folded towels .. OR ... on bricks resting on a bath towel in a few inches of water. Water will pass through the bricks to the plants .. OR ... water them just as you're leaving and cover each with a plastic bag.

- Split leaf philodendrons thrive on a very diluted once-monthly supplement of skimmed milk powder and water. Use sparingly or a milky odour will develop.

- Dangle your hanging plants from fishing swivels and they'll enjoy all-round exposure to the sun. You'll never have to take them down to rotate them – just give 'em a little push.

- Grow bushier, healthier, greener houseplants without commercial fertilizers. Recent scientific studies have shown that ordinary unflavoured gelatine is a marvellous time-release plant nutrient. Dissolve 1 tbsp. gelatine in 1 cup hot tap water, slowly adding 3 cups cold water to this solution. Water your plants with this concoction once monthly during the prime growing season. Gelatine is a valuable source of organic nitrogen.

14

- Before you hold a funeral for your fuchsia, try this: Hanging fuchsia baskets often have a drip tray attached to the pot. Be sure to remove it, or the plant will become waterlogged and will fare poorly. Poke holes in the bottom of hanging paperboard pots, too – you may have to use an electric drill to pierce the thick board, but this could save your fuchsia's life and restore it to blooming glory.

- Make a cheap terrarium by potting your plants in an old goldfish bowl.

- Make plant pot stands for next-to-nothing – use cottage cheese and yoghurt lids.

- An old teapot makes an excellent watering can for your house plants.

Storage

- Store flower bulbs in egg cartons over winter, labelling each carton. This will keep the bulbs dry and unbroken, and you'll know at a glance how many of each type you have.

- Hold a ball of twine neatly in your workshop by tacking an empty mesh fruit basket to the wall. The twine unwinds through the plastic mesh .. OR ... store it in an old teapot, unwinding through the spout.

- Don't throw out that leaky garden hose! Stomp on it with your spiked golf shoes, and turn it into a trickle hose, capping the open end with the top of a vinegar bottle or bleach bottle.

14

- Thieves won't be tempted to steal your brand new garden hose if you wind electrician's tape around it here and there. If they think the hose is leaky, they won't want it.

- Store your garden hose inside an old tyre .. OR ... around a metal tyre rim.

- Keep garden tools tidy, even when space is limited. Slip the handles through lengths of drain pipe bracketed to the wall of your tool-shed or garage.

And Other Gardener's Secrets

- Sweet peas like warm – not cold – water.

- Clematis and other flowering creepers will love the occasional drink of very diluted milk. Swish some water into an empty milk bottle or carton, pouring it at the base of your climber instead of down your sink. Good to the very last drop.

- Flowering creepers also love a beer bath. Rinse out the empty bottles, pouring these very diluted drops of beer over them.

- Roses will smell sweeter, say some gardeners, if you plant parsley beside them.

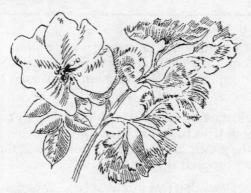

- Ripen late tomatoes right on the vine. Hang the whole plant – roots, stems, and fruit – upside down from a basement rafter, allowing the tomatoes to drop when

14

they're ready. Pillow their fall onto something soft over which you've spread old newspapers, and they won't bruise. Using this method, you're less likely to forget about the fruit than you would be if it ripened in a paper bag.

- To keep your planting rows straight, stretch a string very taut, walking over it; plant in its indentation.

- Vegetable gardens planted north to south thrive better than those planted east to west.

- If an old stump starts to sprout new growth, treat it with a strong saltpetre solution, which will rot it down, or with chlorine bleach, which will stop its renewal. Either way, drill a few holes into it, first.

- Make inexpensive plant markers using lolly sticks.

- Stake drooping plants with strips cut from worn tights or plastic bread bags. They won't cut or break tender plant stalks like cord.

- Plastic plant labels will endure any weather. Cut an old bleach bottle to label size, punching a hole in one end of each label, to tie it to the plant. One cut-up bottle does an average garden, but make sure it's well washed out before you start.

14

Festive Occasions

Christmas

- Your Christmas tree will stay green longer and will not drop its needles if you mix up this solution that florists and tree farmers use. Stir well together 1 gal. hot water, 2 cups golden syrup, 4 tbsp. micronized iron (available at garden shops and nurseries), 4 tsp. liquid bleach. Pour into a large plastic tub or bucket and allow your tree to stand in this overnight, so that it will absorb as much as possible. Then mount tree as usual, making sure you add water as you normally would, keeping branches and needles moist.

- Hang Christmas tree ornaments with inverted paper clips. Why spend money on special hooks?

- Your artificial Christmas tree will assemble faster if you coat the end of each twig with petroleum jelly before inserting it into the base.

- Try these unusual snowflakes on your tree. Poke cocktail sticks all round small Styrofoam balls, for a porcupine effect. Then spray the prickly critters with artificial snow, looping a small string onto the ball so it can be dangled from the tree.

- Wrap small Christmas gifts for pennies – use festive serviettes.

- Wrap large awkward ones, too – use a Christmas paper tablecloth.

- You'll know exactly how much gift wrap to measure if you go once around the parcel with a length of string, first.

- Christmas gifts will be safe from prying eyes if they're

15

116

stored in unused luggage. Who'd ever think to peek there?

- Berried holly looks fresh and festive if it's sprayed with a protective coating of vegetable oil.

- This Christmas bell door decoration costs only a few pence. Spray two small plastic yoghurt containers gold or silver, threading velvet ribbon and a couple of small round tree baubles into the base of each carton. Tie them together so one hangs lower than its mate, and there you have it.

- Make your own Christmas candles with recycled paraffin wax – add a few wax crayons for colour.

- Want to keep your Christmas ribbons tidy and organized? Stand each roll upright in a box that once held foil or wax paper, cutting small slits to pull each colour through.

- Homemade biscuits and sweets make special gifts when they're specially presented. For something different, tuck several in each compartment of the bottom half of an egg carton, decorated with paint, rickrack braid and cardboard wheels, just like a wagon.

- Homemade sweets make a festive gift presented in small squares of Christmas wrapping paper rather than paper cases. Leftover paper is cheaper than little papercases, too.

- Arrange gift biscuits and sweets on well-washed Styrofoam meat trays – makes a perfect backer, especially covered in foil.

- What about these inexpensive gift ideas? Toffee, fudge, and small jars of jam and marmalade can be made at any time and are always appreciated. Bulk lavender can be sewn into sachets and trimmed with bits of lace. Dried flaked parsley, mint, or celery leaves, bottled and beribboned, all have the personal touch. And youngsters enjoy felt-backed bookmarks decorated with rickrack braid, as well as hand-sewn doll clothes and homemade apple dolls.

15

- Moisten dry fruit cakes flavourfully. Using a poultry skewer, poke holes over the top of the cake, pouring a few spoonfuls of your favourite grog inside and wrapping in a rum- or brandy-soaked cloth.

- Fruit cakes have more punch if you soak all cut-up fruits in brandy, sherry, or rum for a couple of days before combining with your recipe.

- Fruits and nuts won't sink to the bottom of your Christmas cakes if you coat them with part of the flour before you add them to your recipe.

- Christmas cranberries need less sugar when you add ¼ tsp. bicarbonate of soda to the cooking water.

- Leftover eggnog makes a lovely sauce for vanilla ice cream or cake. And mixed with rice, it makes a tasty rice pudding. Just substitute it for the milk in your recipe.

- Pamper your poinsettia and enjoy its bloom another Christmas. But bringing back those blooms takes patience and perseverance.

    Allow your plant plenty of sunlight over the festive season – a window location is ideal. Move it away from the window's cold drafts each night. Let it drink lukewarm water rather than cold, ensuring that the pot never gets "wet feet" and that the saucer underneath it is drained immediately.

    When leaves and coloured bracts begin falling in February or March, move the plant to a cool, light base-

15

118

ment and allow it to dry out almost completely between waterings. In April, prune the plant so all stems are no longer than 3 inches; the pruned parts can be repotted to start more plants.

Transplant your pruned poinsettia into a pot filled with fresh soil, giving it just a little water and moving it to a sunny location where temperatures remain moderate. Thin the shoots it produces until no more than three or four remain, burying the pot in the garden in mid-June. Your poinsettia will enjoy the morning sun, but not the afternoon's; water and feed it outdoors until autumn.

Now here's where you really get serious. Bring the plant indoors in the autumn, giving it a nightly 12 to 14 hours of total, uninterrupted darkness around Oct. 10. It needs plenty of light by day, but anything less than complete nightly darkness – even briefly – may keep it from flowering at Christmas.

- Stuff a turkey and stow the mess. Open both ends of a well-washed soup or juice can, spooning the stuffing through it .. OR ... heap the stuffing into a square of cheesecloth that has been folded over three or four times. Tie the ends in a knot and pop the bag directly into your turkey, chicken, or goose, lifting it out when you're ready to carve. You'll have plenty of hot stuffing, ready for a bowl, while your bird will be clean as a whistle.

- Poultry stuffings will have a fine nut-like flavour if you add a handful of uncooked rolled oats to the mixture.

- Make company canapes from leftover turkey stuffing, combining scooped-out cherry tomatoes and mushrooms with it and baking until golden.

- Your turkey will baste itself if you drape it with a single layer of cheesecloth and lay a few bacon slices over that. The fat from the bacon adds flavour to the gravy, and the few bits stuck to the cloth can be added to the stuffing.

- Your turkey will also baste itself if you cook the stuffing separately and stand a cooking apple in its cavity.

- Beat the Christmas crunch – those last few minutes before

15

119

mealtime when you're expected to dish up half a dozen fancy dishes, serving everything hot while you pretend to be cool. So here's a sneaky way to actually be as organized as you're attempting to appear. Make the sauce for your plum pudding in the morning, pouring it into a vacuum flask that has been preheated with boiling water. Your sauce will be piping hot when dessert time comes, with no pot to scour.

Birthdays

- Birthday cakes are twice the fun if you use coloured sweets or marshmallows as candle holders.

- Trim a youngster's birthday cake with popped corn. It's unusual and it's fun, easily adhering to the sides of an iced cake.

- Inflate short-necked party balloons more easily with the aid of a ballpoint pen cap. Cut the tip off the cap, snapping the neck of the balloon over the wider end, and puff.

- Why mortgage your home to buy birthday party trinkets that so often have one less in the package than the number of children at your party? Save the prizes at the bottom of your breakfast cereal for just such occasions – assuming the kids don't get them first.

- Be inventive when you wrap gifts. The weekend coloured comics make a brightly festive wrap for children's presents; leftover wallpaper is bright and interesting; a

15

detailed map is just the thing in which to wrap a bon voyage gift.

■ Don't spend precious pennies on fireplace matches. Light a strand of raw spaghetti. It will burn beautifully, and makes a great lighter for birthday cakes, too. The thin kind works best.

Easter and Hallowe'en

■ Colour Easter eggs without a costly dye kit. Boiled onion skins produce light yellow eggs; grass and crushed leaves will turn eggs green; beets result in scarlet pink.

■ Save money when you buy chocolate chips after Easter – buy half-price chocolate bunnies and chicks, crushing them yourself.

■ Enjoy your Hallowe'en jack-o-lantern all year long. The insides make delicious loaves and pies if you know how. Scraping off any burned portions and blobs of wax, cut your pumpkin shell into large chunks and bake it on a baking sheet at about 400 deg. F. for 45 min. Scoop the cooled pulp into a blender, pureeing until smooth. Package, label, and freeze.

15

General Party Tips

■ Need a large salad bowl for a crowd? Use your punch bowl.

- Jot down each menu served to guests, file at the back of your recipe box, and you'll always have combinations that work within easy reach. You also won't run the risk of repeating dishes when the same friends call.

- Keep a supply of party foods such as tinned smoked oysters and shrimp in a special place in your cupboard, and you'll always be ready for unexpected visitors.

- Patty shells are expensive party food – but not if you make your own this simple way. Cut 2-inch-thick slices of French bread, hollowing out the centres of each slice. Fry in deep fat until golden brown, drain on paper towelling, and heap with the filling of your choice.

- Why buy party ice cubes? Freeze extra a couple of days ahead, popping them out of their trays and into brown paper bags. Repeat until you have enough. The cubes won't stick to the paper bag; they do stick to plastic.

- Make party ice cubes special by popping a maraschino cherry into each as it's freezing. This is pretty in a punch bowl.

- Candles will drip less if you soak them in salt water (2 tbsp. salt per candle and enough water to cover) before lighting.

- Candles will burn more slowly if you store them in the freezer between uses.

- Straighten droopy candles by rolling them in a flat-bottomed pan filled with warm water, hardening them again by plunging them into a pan of cold water.

15

122

- Candles that are too small for their holders will fit snugly if you wrap an elastic band around the last half-inch of their base .. OR ... if you allow some of the melted wax to drop to the bottom of the holder first, quickly inserting the candle and allowing it to set in the wax.

- Candles that are too large for their holders will fit snugly if you soften the base slightly by dipping it in boiling water for a few seconds.

15

And The Rest

Posting Parcels

- Cushion small delicate objects in the mail by padding with a couple of bath sponges, polystyrene, or foam chips.

- Packages will tie more snugly if you dampen the string first. As it dries, it contracts.

- Not enough glue on envelopes and stamps? Seal your letters with a few dabs of clear nailpolish.

- Separate stuck postage stamps by popping them into the freezer overnight – the glue will still be usable, too!

- Mailed packages are more likely to reach their destination if you protect the name and address of the recipient with clear Sellotape and enclose a slip of paper in the package with the address of both sender and recipient.

Lost and Found

- No more forgotten messages – glue a strip of Velcro to your phone and another to your pen.

- Store seldom-used bedding in seldom-used luggage.

- Store photo negatives behind the pictures in your album.

- Store a fishing rod neatly by gluing or screwing two clothes pegs to a wall stud or ceiling. The pegs clip the rod.

- Store fish hooks securely in your tackle box by gluing a block of Styrofoam to the inside of the lid.

16

- Store rings and bracelets on a cuphook mounted beside the kitchen sink – you'll never misplace your valuables as you cook and clean.

- Retrieve objects from hard-to-reach places by snapping a sock to the end of a cane (use an elastic band) to extend your reach.

- Fish for lost metal items by taping a strong powerful magnet to a straightened coat hanger.

- Lose the tip of your umbrella? Replace it with a toothpaste cap.

Looking After Valuables

- The safest place for your precious gems remains a safety deposit box, but if you have more rings than fingers and worry when your gems are unguarded, pop each into an ice cube tray and freeze. No one will guess you've got a fortune on ice!

- Hide small valuables such as earrings and brooches in a small magnetic car key box, fastened to your bed frame.

- Photocopy your credit cards and stash the information in your safety deposit box.

Beating the Cold Weather

- Free frozen locks by holding a match or lighter under your key.

16

- Thaw frozen pipes by wrapping an electric blanket around them.

- Snow will slide off a shovel sprayed with furniture polish or vegetable oil.

- It's easy to find your favourite electric blanket setting even in total darkness. Tape a small strip of adhesive over the numbered setting at which you feel most comfortable, and you'll notice the spots at once, even when the lights are off.

- Heat a cold bed even when the family's only hot water bottle is already in use. Rely on grandma's favourite method: Let a brick warm slowly at the back of the stove or in your oven, wrapping it in a towel when you're ready to retire.

Calculations Made Easy

- If metric meat prices flummox you, remember this trick. Divide the price per kilogram by two, subtracting 10 per cent from the result. That will give you the price per pound, and a little piece of mind.

- To convert kilometres to miles, multiply everything but the last digit by 6. Example 50 km = 30 miles because $5 \times 6 = 30$, and 100 km = 60 miles because $10 \times 6 = 60$.

- To convert Fahrenheit to Celsius, subtract 32 from your Fahrenheit temperature and multiply the result by $5/9$. That's $F - 32 \times 5/9 = C$. Example: 68 deg. F. = 20 deg. C. because $68 - 32 = 36 \times 5/9 = 20$.

- To convert Celsius to Fahrenheit, the reverse applies: $9/5$ Deg. C. $+ 32 = F$. Example: To convert 20 deg. C. to Fahrenheit, take $9/5 \times 20 = 36 + 32 = 68$. Simple, isn't it? Well, I don't think so, either.

Postscript

- You'll know when you're about to run out of staples if you run a stripe of red nailpolish across the last few in the stapler.

- Cut slices from a pencil eraser to make "feet" for vibrating clocks and slippery ashtrays.

- The finger of an old rubber glove is an ideal applicator for paste or glue.

- Rubber gloves slip on and off more easily with a little talc sprinkled inside.

- Playing cards won't stick if they're lightly dusted with talcum powder.

- Revive tired tennis balls by wrapping them individually in foil and heating ½ hour in a 200 degree F. oven to restore lost bounce. They can be reheated several times over when they become droopy again.

- Revive listless ping-pong balls by pouring boiling water over them.

- Make a simple bookmark and avoid turned-down pages. Use the snipped corner of an envelope.

- Straighten warped records by placing between two panes of glass and leaving several hours in the hot sun.

Index

H

Hair,
    conditioning, 73-4
    washing, 74
Halitosis, 77
Hallowe'en, 121
Handyman helpers, 53-62
Hangover cures, 81
Headaches, 78
Heat marks on furniture, 68
Haemorrhoids, 78
Hems, to remove mark, 65
Hiccups, 77
Hot Chocolate, to make, 49
Hot weather tips, 75

I

Ink stains,
    on desk, 65
    on fabrics, 65
    on leather or vinyl, 63
Iodine stains, 66
Insect repellents, 95
Insomnia, 78
Iron, cleaning, 18
Ironing tips, 35
Itching, 34

J

Jewellery,
    to clean, 72
    to restring necklace, 72
    to store, 125

K

Kettles, to clean, 18
Kitchen floors, to clean, 21
Knife blades, to clean, 16
Knitting, 90

L

Ladders, to steady and make
    safer, 59

Lampshades, to clean, 28
Laundry, general tips, 33
Leather, to clean, 27
Leftovers, 48
Lemons,
    squeeze extra juice, 42
    to store, 42
Lettuce,
    to grow faster, 102
    to revive, 40
Lice, 97
Light bulbs, to replace, 60
Lipstick,
    to remove stains, 66
    to save money, 76
Lost items, 23

M

Make-up stains, 66
Marble, to clean, 24
Margarine,
    to soften, 44
    to whip, 44
Marshmallows,
    as candleholders, 120
    to cut, 50
Measuring tape, 61
Meat,
    leftovers, 37
    organizing in freezer, 17
    separating frozen burgers, 38
    to tenderize, 38
Medical remedies, 77-83
Medicine, to swallow more
    easily, 83
Metric conversions made easy,
    120
Microwave ovens,
    to clean, 13
    to dry flowers, 110
Mildew,
    on books, 66
    on canvas, 66
    on other fabrics, 66
    on leather, 66
    on walls, 24
    on washable fabrics, 66